From: <u>Carol Tipler with pen name, Anne Ravenoak</u>, author of The Storyteller and his Story, Marten River Hideaway, The Returning, Secrets of the Bluebird Inn, Gentle Annie, and Touring With Merri, lives in North Bay, Ontario, with her husband.

"THIS IS A WINNER! This is a striking and poignant story that Hay House will EMBRACE."

<u>Her review:</u>

"Forget The Handmaid's Tale or Fifty Shades of Grey. Fantasy cannot hold a candle to the real world of *Because I Didn't Tell*.

Katchastarr (pseudonym) writes of her traumatic experiences of abuse and incest with forthright detail that keeps the reader intensely involved in her story. It is at once an emotionally clearing venue for the author and a manual to help others escape from their victimization. Victims must realize that they should not feel guilty or ashamed, the author points out; they must speak out to protect themselves.

Throughout her story, one thing is clear: Misogyny is alive and flourishing. Thirty years ago and even today, the words of a pathological liar often took and still take precedence over a victim's statements. People hesitate to speak up about abuse, either as a victim or as a witness, because they find it difficult to face up to their own vulnerabilities or culpabilities.

The author's love for her parents, especially her mom, stands out, and she realizes her deep-seated need to please her parents and siblings. It came as a shock to realize that her parents were only human with human frailties. They supported her as much as they could, yet a comment from her dad led to a distancing which took her a long time to recover from.

As well, agencies that are supposed to be there to support victims often fall short of their goal and cause more problems than they solve. In the final analysis, the journey Katchastarr took to overcome her adversities was rough, but she emerged triumphant, and, she tells her readers, they can triumph too.

Because I Didn't Tell is a must-read for anyone, victim or not.

<u>From: Barbara Anello Bsc, MBA, OMC</u>

"I finished my first read-through of your amazing manuscript. Although it initially triggered me, I can honestly admit that it was incredibly cathartic ... perhaps it's because time, experience, and wisdom have helped heal me through this journey.

Your book, Because I Didn't Tell, and how powerfully you detailed the gratitude and pearls of wisdom lifted me up and made my spirit soar.

YOUR manuscript helped me relive my experiences in a different light… that made it wonderful.

I identified very much with your struggles and I know we are not alone in what we've survived. xoxox

I never met anyone before who articulated, as well as you have, a different perspective... and how much better off you are that you forgave so you could move forward.

Bless you beautiful."

*In June 1995, Barbara Anello was recognized by the Ministry of Culture and Citizenship as a recipient for the prestigious **Ontario Medal for Good Citizenship** for her work in pioneering prevention initiatives in the brain injury movement.*

BECAUSE I DIDN'T TELL

I. KATCHASTARR

BALBOA.
PRESS

A DIVISION OF HAY HOUSE

Balboa Press books may be ordered through booksellers or by contacting:

Balboa Press
A Division of Hay House
1663 Liberty Drive
Bloomington, IN 47403
www.balboapress.com
1 (877) 407-4847

Because of the dynamic nature of the Internet, any web addresses or links contained in this book may have changed since publication and may no longer be valid. The views expressed in this work are solely those of the author and do not necessarily reflect the views of the publisher, and the publisher hereby disclaims any responsibility for them.

The author of this book does not dispense medical advice or prescribe the use of any technique as a form of treatment for physical, emotional, or medical problems without the advice of a physician, either directly or indirectly. The intent of the author is only to offer information of a general nature to help you in your quest for emotional and spiritual well-being. In the event you use any of the information in this book for yourself, which is your constitutional right, the author and the publisher assume no responsibility for your actions.

Any people depicted in stock imagery provided by Thinkstock are models, and such images are being used for illustrative purposes only. Certain stock imagery © Thinkstock.

Printed in Canada

ISBN: 978-1-5043-8392-9 (sc)
ISBN: 978-1-5043-8394-3 (hc)
ISBN: 978-1-5043-8393-6 (e)

Library of Congress Control Number: 2017910514

Balboa Press rev. date: 08/14/2017

CONTENTS

PRELUDE

I trust and truly believe that everything that has happened to me, and my family, had a purpose. I am valuing my self-worth, and that of my children, by sharing these events with the sincere purpose to honor our lives … *not* what has happened to us.

We are all so precious and worthy of all good things. I believe and embrace this, and I am forever grateful for the people, my God, the angels, the spirits, the archangels, and the divine intervention that supported me as I transitioned from a helpless, fear-filled victim to a fearless, faith-filled, free-spirited survivor and *thriver*!

This is my story based on the details of my life.

I have changed the dates, the names of places, and the names of people to respect their privacy. I have deliberately *italicized* words such as *he, him,* and *his* in order to identify my abuser and to *not* glorify *him* by giving *him* a name … other than Phidelopé (fictional name).

I cherish the angelic voice in my right ear that whispered to me: "*He's* only as strong, threatening, and evil as the words from *his* mouth that you choose to *believe*!"

I decided then to believe what I have always felt in my soul: that there is good in everyone. I realized that *he* was just really sick, and I could not help *him*. I gave *him* back to God.

I remember thinking to myself: It really won't matter if *he* kills our children, my family, and me, because *his* violent actions (that we were repeatedly subjected to) invasively stole our innocence and killed a part of me deep within my soul.

CHAPTER 1

———— ❖ ————

Rape

On a crisp mid-November evening in 1981, I decided to invite my ex-boyfriend to my place for a friendly dinner. We had been apart for several months, and Phidelopé and his family were the only familiar people in this new city. I had moved there to pursue my employment because my previous employer had upgraded to computers. I was the last person to be hired, so I was the first employee to be dismissed during the company's downsizing.

During a phone conversation, Phidelopé and I spoke briefly about this upcoming dinner, and we both agreed it was with the intention to remain just friends. I clearly chose not to have *him* as a boyfriend, although, at that time, I enjoyed spending time with *him* and his family.

Another intention was to quietly celebrate my nineteenth birthday. My family had been away for my actual birthday because they were moose hunting; the hunt always fell over the weeks that included my birthday. Their hunt was successful, and they shared some of the moose meat with me. Phidelopé was anxious to taste the wild meat, as *he* had never had such an experience before. So this was my plan. We would share a simple, friendly dinner and evening of conversation to begin a friendship-only relationship.

1

The dinner did go well. We each had one glass of white wine, as neither of us really liked it. But since I was finally of legal age to drink, I thought we could experience a nice glass of wine.

Our evening ended early, around eight o'clock. I walked Phidelopé to the door and said, "Good night."

As I was closing the door, suddenly I felt *him* pushing the door back toward me. At first I thought *he* was being silly, so I pushed back gently. Then, *he* pushed back with all his might! I vividly remember the look on Phidelopé's face as *his* eyes changed, and I didn't recognize this person anymore. I remember the sound of a loud bang as the bright-orange wooden door slammed against the wall.

I felt shocked and completely powerless as *he* brutally picked me up and rushed me straight down the hallway into my bedroom. Phidelopé flung me onto my single bed, and I remember wondering, *What on earth is going on?* In no time at all, it felt as though *he* had eight hands, and they were all over me. On top of me, Phidelopé weighed a ton. I felt frightened, overwhelmed, bewildered, and totally helpless as my pants were ripped off my body. The heavy weight of *his* body pressed against mine. I suddenly realized I was being raped.

I took a deep breath and screamed, "Rape!"

Phidelopé looked at me with *his* vicious cold, criminal eyes. I screamed once more, this time as loudly as I possibly could. "Rape!"

Then, in an instant, *he* slammed his whole right arm into my mouth, jarring it open and effectively keeping me voiceless. In another flash, *his* left fist connected with the right temple area of my head. That pounding smack knocked me unconscious.

Ring, ring, ring, ring. The sound of my telephone echoed in my ears. Very faintly at first as I simultaneously physically felt my soul slip back into my body. It was a bizarre feeling; it felt as though everything was happening in slow motion. Once I collected myself enough to realize I was hearing the phone ring, I became conscious of myself in my body. Everything ached. I was freezing, naked, and shaking tremendously as I pulled myself into a standing position. Overwhelmed with weakness, I crawled to the telephone. I answered with a shaky, "Hello."

When I heard the voice of the office manager at the bank where I worked, I knew I was late. A quick glance at the clock told me I was late by half an hour already. She asked if I was coming into work on that messed-up Monday morning in November. Without a blink, I said yes and apologized for being late. I told her I would be there within the hour.

I remember feeling panicked about being late for work. And for the first time in my life, I couldn't remember why I was running late. I looked around and saw my apartment door was wide open, my room was in shambles, and my clothes were scattered on the floor. I stood there, shaking. My naked body trembled. Beaten and shocked, I stared in disbelief at what I saw. I pulled myself into the shower. My aching body still felt the aftermath from the events that I was trying to remember.

The throbbing, aching pain in my vagina and pelvic area and my pounding, swollen head quickly painted the picture for me. I began to sob and cry with the realization of what I had been through. Frightened, alone, and uncertain of the next steps to take, my higher consciousness knew I needed to report this, and I should get to the hospital. The shock to my body, the insult to my soul, the brutal theft of my innocence, and the disgust I felt for myself kept me in that shower, scrubbing, crying, cleaning my whole self until the water ran cold. The shock of the cold water reminded me of my commitment to get to work within the hour. I recited in my head,

You have to get to work. You have to pay your bills and your rent. You are responsible for yourself. Now pull yourself together and go to work.

I gathered myself, got dressed, and walked the two miles to work. To this day, I don't remember feeling myself walk all those steps to the front door and enter my place of employment. I just happened to get there. I settled myself behind my teller's wicket. I didn't tell a soul about what happened. I carried on with my day for the purpose of putting the whole event behind me.

I kept to myself those following weeks, healing my aching body; tending to self-care; installing a bolt lock, chain lock, and new key lock to the door of my apartment; and praying I would never see *him* again.

During this time, I was also going through orthodontic treatment and had recently had my braces adjusted. I thought that was probably the reason for the migraines I was beginning to experience, and the migraines were probably what was making me feel sick to my stomach. But because I kept feeling sick, I thought perhaps I had a flu bug. I set up an appointment with Phidelopé's family's physician, as I was new to the city and didn't have one for myself. The physician was kind and happy to know I was a friend of Phidelopé's family. He took my health history, checked for fever, took blood and urine samples, and suggested I take some antinausea medication to settle my stomach. The doctor also told me to rest as necessary. I didn't take any time away from work. I knew it was important to maintain a normal way of living, because my family was counting on me to be the young adult woman I promised them I would be.

One day as I walked home from work, my arms loaded down with the weight of six grocery bags, a car horn honked behind me. My parents always told me to never acknowledge anyone whistling or honking at me, so I ignored it. With my head held high, I continued to walk on. I felt the car slow down next to me, and I heard the smooth slide of a window coming down as the car slowed almost to a stop next to me. Then I heard Phidelopé's voice. I immediately felt weak as that voice echoed through my head, hearing *him* shout, "Hey, stop! I need to talk to you."

I kept walking, my head still held high, trying to ignore *his* unwelcome presence. *He* persisted, and at the corner of the next street, Phidelopé pulled in front of me and put his car in park. When I turned to look, I was shocked to see *his* prized, pearl-handled gun, which was passed down to *him* from *his* grandfather, lying on the passenger seat. Phidelopé purposely positioned *his* hand close to it as *he* leaned sideways to look at me through the passenger-side window.

"Get in the car," *he* said. "We need to talk."

Clutched with fear and feeling vulnerable and alone, crazy thoughts raced through my mind. *This man just raped me. What would stop him from killing me with that pearl-handled gun he's so proud of?* I was sure I was going to die. Like a zombie or someone having an out-of-body experience, I found myself opening the door to the back seat of *his* car, throwing the grocery bags onto the back seat, and opening the front door to slide in and surrender to *his* imprisonment. I sat there, motionless and terrified, as *he* told me how I would live out the rest of my days.

His opening statement was, "Hey, guess what? You're pregnant!"

I remember turning my head in shock, looking straight into *his* eyes, and saying, "Pardon me? You're telling me I'm pregnant! How would you know such a thing?"

I'll never forget the look on his face as *he* stared right back at me with a snarly smile on *his* face, Mr. Know-it-all, saying, "Well, you went to see our family doctor, didn't you?"

Then I remembered. *Oh my God! Yes, I did!*

He then said, "I called to get the results."

In shock, I asked, "Results ... of what? How? What do you mean?"

Once more, that smug smile came across his face as *he* glared at me and told me that *he* told the family physician we were trying to conceive, and *he* was anxious to find out if our efforts had been successful so *he* could tell me if I was pregnant. The doctor didn't question this, so he told *him*, "Yes, as a matter fact, Itzabella is pregnant."

The shock of what *he* could do vibrated through my whole being. I asked *him*, "What? Are you stalking me?" Which was a silly question, because the question was the answer ... of course *he* was!

Again, the smug smile came across *his* face as *he* began to inform me how we were going to spend the rest of our days together.

I remember looking around at the surroundings—the traffic zooming past us, the mall across the street from us—and thinking, "I need to run ... I need to tell ... I need to get away!" Yet, I was paralyzed with fear in that seat in *his* car with *his* eyes piercing through my soul. *His* lips were moving, and the words were flowing yet, I didn't really understand the depth of what I was surrendering my soul, my unborn child, and myself too.

He began by telling me that if I didn't accept any of the conditions that *he* presented to me while waiving the pearl handled gun in front of me, though out of view of any passersby, that *he* would kill me. Without looking at *him*, staring blankly into space, I listened as the tears rolled down my face.

I remember *him* insisting that we were going to get married. I remember hearing *him* say, "If you don't marry me, I will kill you. If you don't marry me and decide to have the baby, I will take the baby from you. If you abort the baby, I will kill you. If you do have the baby and try to run away from me, I will find you and I will kill you. If you tell anybody, *anybody*, the truth about our circumstances and this pregnancy, I will kill you, and I will kill them."

He went on to say, "If you tell your family and they try to charge me with rape and try to keep you and this baby away from me, I will kill your entire family!"

I knew *he* was serious about all of these threats. All that I could remember then was the violent circumstances of the recent event that now put me where I am—pregnant and enduring more threats from this horrible, disturbed young man. The words *you're pregnant* spun through my head, and all of a sudden the flu-like symptoms that I was experiencing made sense to me. I was having morning sickness. The migraines, more than likely, were the result of the blow to my head that had knocked me unconscious for hours. The foggy rerun of the traumatic event came through to me, and I realized that this man had left me for dead—the door wide open, my naked body on my bed, my clothes torn off of me, and thrown around my room. *He* did this to me so I believed, right there and then, that *he* could follow through with any or all the threats that *he* had just uttered to me. I surrendered. I felt powerless, and I desperately clung to the new life that was growing inside of me. I remember telling myself that my life was no longer about me; it was about this living, little, innocent person growing inside of me. I dedicated myself, at that very moment, to being the best mom I could ever be and to never blame this child for what happened. I told myself this child was a miracle and somehow my blessing.

Because I didn't tell anyone about the horrific circumstances that rendered me pregnant, or anything about the surreal silent contract that I now held with this monster of a man, *he* now controlled my future. The months passed by quickly. I continued to work every day as scheduled. I was amazed as I watched my body changing, always reassuring my unborn child with whispers of, "Mommy loves you, and I will take good care of you."

This quiet ritual was also my prayer to myself, as I was terrified of this man and this fear made me *his* prisoner. I would do everything I could in order to keep *him* from killing this unborn child, my family, and me.

As Christmas approached, *he* told me how we would talk to my family about my condition and how we would become engaged to be married at their home during the Christmas holiday. We would share with them the wedding date that we had in mind: March 6, 1982.

I now forgive myself for:

- My naivety
- Deciding to be *his* friend
- Not reporting the rape to police
- Taking a shower and going to work instead of going to the hospital immediately upon regaining consciousness.
- Agreeing to *his* terms.

PEARL OF WISDOM

Forgiveness allows me to heal and be peaceful as I move forward in life. It does not mean that what happened is okay. I value the lesson, and I leave the experience behind.

CHAPTER 2

Why Me?

In the months that followed, I began to think, *Who am I? Why is this happening to me, now?*

I remember being curled up in my bed, necessarily refreshed with newly purchased blankets, pillows, and pillowcases, and thinking to myself, *I'm a smart young lady. I grew up within a happy, healthy family. I have wonderful friends. The people appreciate me in my hometown. I have a bright future ahead of me. How did all of this change?*

Then I realized that right from the time I met Phidelopé my plans for my future were altered.

I met *him* shortly after my return home from the university that I attended in New Brunswick. I chose to take this time for myself, to mature, as I had just turned seventeen during my first semester there. My decision was prompted from being overwhelmed with university-level calculus.

While I was attending university, in my endeavor to overcome my struggle with calculus, I sought a recommendation from university counselors for a tutor on campus. When I got to the dorm room, this wonderful, tall young man from the island of Cuba invited me in, and we discussed the terms of his tutorship. Then he introduced me to his roommate, J.P. We smiled at each other as we said hello.

My tutor stepped out of the room for a moment, leaving me with J.P. In seconds, this young, handsome man got uncomfortably close to me during our conversation. It was fun, at first, and interesting; yet, I wondered when his roommate would return. Before I knew it, J.P. had his hands on my shoulders, then one hand moved to my thigh, and then he leaned in to kiss me. I remember feeling frightened and praying for the tutor to return. I felt his thick lips over mine, and I remember squirming away from the weight of his body, reaching for and opening the door and wildly running to my dorm room. I vowed then to never go back to that tutor, and because I didn't tell the university authorities about this incident, I chose instead to dismiss myself from the Bachelor of Science program that I had such high hopes of achieving. I was grateful for the university's kind and generous offer to honor my scholarship upon my return the following September, but that never happened.

Upon my return home I remember feeling the shock and disappointment of my family and the entire community that I, Super Smart Itzabella, had failed to accomplish my dream. I felt equally as disappointed and ashamed of myself, and I surrendered to the terms of my return.

My parents clearly stated that if I was to stay at home, I needed to find a job and pay a minimal rent. I got a job at a lumber mill. I totally disliked the work, the odor of the chemicals used to treat the wood, and the work hours; yet, I continued to do so in order to fulfill my commitment to my family. I was wise enough to seek other employment during my days off, and within a week, I received a call from the local bank. I thought it was a mistake because I didn't have an account at that bank; the payroll for the lumber mill went straight to a credit union in our town. The manager, over the phone, explained that my summertime employer from the general grocery store had referred me to him. I was grateful for this recommendation and quickly accepted an interview. I was happy to get the job on the spot. During the application and hire process, the manager laughed out loud as she realized that my current age of seventeen didn't qualify for the employee credit card that each new employee was granted once hired. I didn't mind, as I preferred not to have a credit card at that time.

I met *him* at a house party that I chose to attend with my sister, as I welcomed her friendship; we were not always the best of friends while growing up together. Phidelopé was funny and polite, and I could sense that *he* was much more excited about meeting me than I was about meeting *him*; however, I endured our polite conversation. I was stunned and surprised the next day when the whistling of *his* car horn honking announced *his* presence. *He* had installed a specific car horn that mimicked the sound of a man whistling to get a female's attention. *He* pulled up next to me while I was walking along the boulevard. *He* expressed to me *his* excitement about finding me and noted that *he* was visiting *his* grandparents who lived in the same community where I was living, for now, with my parents. I kept on with the plans that I made for myself for that day rather than agreeing to spend the day with *him* driving around town in *his* truck.

The following weekend, I was surprised to see *him* at a dance where my sister, some other girlfriends and I were enjoying the music. *He* showed up with a handsome friend. They asked if they could join us at our table, and we granted them permission. I was delighted when this handsome young man named Derrick asked me to dance. I could see from the corner of my eye, the glare of disapproval from Phidelopé as *he* sat at the table with my sister and our friends. I danced a few more times with Derrick, and when he asked permission to walk me home, I gratefully accepted.

The following day I received a phone call from Phidelopé expressing *his* disapproval of my choice to walk home with *his* friend Derrick. I thought this was strange, and I laughed out loud as I expressed my bewilderment with *his* disapproval. I remember thinking to myself that I wasn't really pleased with this display of behavior.

Not surprisingly, Derrick soon moved away to Calgary, Alberta, and I never saw him again. Years later, I found out that Derrick was convinced to move out west by *him*.

This was the beginning of our relationship—dating on weekends when *he* would visit *his* grandparents. We continued with this long-distance relationship for a few months; however, *his* odd behavior and alarming control of me and my choices led me to the decision to call off our relationship.

One particular event that defined *his* odd behavior unfolded during a visit at my parents' place. *He* was pacing from window to window as *he* excitedly watched two of our neighborhood dogs copulating. The bulge in *his* pants clearly indicated the level of *his* excitement, and a red flag went up for me when *he* quickly dialed *his* grandparents' phone number to share the details of what *he* was watching with *his* grandfather. My mother and I looked at each other in disbelief of what was happening. Such strange behavior for a grown man— correction: two grown men.

I can still remember the relief I felt when I chose to break up with *him* shortly after that incident. Never in my dreams did I think *he* could become the man whose behavior would haunt me for the rest of my life.

I now forgive myself for:

- Not reporting the incident to university authorities
- Leaving university and my dream behind
- Not honoring my self-worth

PEARL OF WISDOM

People show you who they are. Believe what they are showing you. Don't let what you hope or think is "love" blind you. *Intuition* has three *Is* ... all the better to see with!

CHAPTER 3

The Wedding

Winter in Northern Ontario and Quebec is picturesque and a fun-filled time for snow lovers. The month of March brought life to our community with the enthusiasm of children building snowmen, having snowball fights, snowshoeing, and tobogganing and families enjoying sleigh rides on snow-covered paths.

March 6, 1982, was an exceptionally harsh winter's day. Snowfall warnings lit up the television screens and blared through radio waves. The flashing blue lights of snowplows lit up the day and continued well into the evening as they rumbled through the hilly streets of Kipming, Quebec, racing to stay ahead of the heavy snowfall.

I prayed for the safety of the travelers from near and far who were making their way to gather at the tiny Catholic church to witness our wedding ceremony. The ceremony was deliberately set for seven o'clock in the evening to avoid having a full-meal reception. Our families were not financially flush, and none of us were prepared for this shotgun wedding.

When I entered the church draped in my marabou-trimmed cape with my hands clenched and warm in my marabou muff, I was surprised at the number of guests who had actually arrived there safely. *What a blessing*, I thought, and I thanked God for answering my prayers. Secretly, I had also prayed that the snowstorm would have been severe enough to cancel our evening wedding ceremony.

The church organ music startled me and magically moved me down the aisle to the altar. The look in my father's moist eyes as he kissed me on the cheek and handed me over to *him* haunts me still. I know he only wanted the best for me, his second little girl. I could feel their eyes watching me; yet, I still cannot remember the faces of the family and friends who welcomed me.

I felt detached from the entire event. I even did my own hair, makeup, and nails earlier that day, feeling like I was preparing myself for a high school prom night. It was all so strange. I felt as though I were hovering overhead, observing the ceremony and the congregation until I heard the priest's voice utter the words, "And you, Itzabella, do you take this man to be your lawfully wedded husband?"

I felt my face flush and my heart pound in my chest, as I was being called in to participate. I slowly gazed at my bridesmaids, my family, *his* family, the gathering of friends, extended family members, and the singer, organist, and altar boys. My eyes glazed over with tears of appreciation for their presence. When I turned to look at *him*, a loud and clear voice resounded in my head repeatedly saying, *No! No! No!*

I could sense how this hesitation was alarming and frustrating *him*, and a fear-filled, "I do," escaped my lips before I knew it.

These two precious words that little girls grow up practicing while playing Barbie doll weddings with their friends and sisters and in their imaginations became the noose around my neck, and *he* was the mighty hangman! I prayed that someone from the congregation would object, but that only happens in the movies. Right?

I resolved to fake a happy marriage in order to keep the peace and to save myself, and our unborn child, from the unimaginable harm *he* could do to us.

I now forgive myself for:

- Accepting and convincing myself, that I had to lie to my parents, *his* parents, our siblings, our friends, our communities, and the priest who married us in order to save lives

PEARL OF WISDOM

Never sign or enter a contract that does not honor your highest good.

CHAPTER 4

Fake It Till You Make It

Hormonal, hot, my gown sticking to my sweaty, tired, aching body, I was anxious for the reception to be over. We smiled as we took turns sitting and having polite brief conversations with our guests. We followed customary wedding reception rituals and danced our first dance alone in front of everyone present. Then I danced with my father alone. To this day, I still cannot recall the songs we chose for these important dances in a Catholic bride's life. I was too worried about what was next … the honeymoon.

We were blessed with enough gifts in the form of cash and checks to cover our flight and motel stay in Florida. We were to spend one week there. We were both nervous about flying, as neither one of us had ever traveled outside of Canada. *He* had a great uncle who lived in Florida whom *he* wanted to visit while we were there. *His* uncle had a new wife, and both men were excited to meet each other's brides. A quick phone call from our hotel room, and they set the date, place, time, and location of where we would meet and eat.

I was happy to feel the warm air and sense the sunshine on my skin. Before I could shower and change into summer clothing, *he* frantically ran from our room to the ice machine numerous times to fill the bathtub with ice. When I asked *him* why *he* did that, *he* looked at me in disbelief and said, "It's for my beer!"

With that, *he* sped off to find a liquor store to buy alcohol and beer. *He* must have made friends with a dealer too, because *he* also came back with a stash of marijuana. Ugh!

I felt frightened and alone in that dingy motel. I dialed the operator and asked her to connect me with my parents' phone in Canada. I really didn't care how much it would cost. I just needed to feel safe and not so sad.

I cried myself to sleep that night, praying that *he'd* be drunk and stoned enough to leave me alone.

We dressed in our nicest clothes the evening that we met *his* great uncle and his new wife. We met at a fancy restaurant, and I was embarrassed when *he* deliberately ordered the most expensive items on the menu. *He* justified this by declaring how rich *his* great uncle was and saying he would want to pay for us to enjoy a nice meal. I was nauseous and hardly ate anything. I shared conversation with his wife, and we both laughed as we noticed an oddly unusual bond between the two men we were married to. They sat close to each other, whispering in each other's ears at times, as they laughed loudly, smoked cigarettes, and drank whiskey.

His great uncle's blue-green eyes locked onto mine as he leaned forward and asked me, "So, how's married life so far?"

I felt nervous and fearful as I desperately wanted to tell someone, *anyone*, the truthful answer to this question, but I didn't. I just smiled and shyly said, "It's okay."

The heat and humidity caused my feet to swell and gave me severe headaches. I didn't have nearly as much fun as *he* did when we visited Disney World. In my condition, I could not experience a lot of the rides. It felt like I was there with my son, not my husband, as *he* impatiently stood in line for *his* favorite wild rides. I took this opportunity to purchase our baby's first gift: a tiny stuffed Goofy.

I would swim in the motel's oval-shaped pool rather than risk being swept away by the ocean waves. *He* preferred the beach and all the lovely ladies draped, nearly naked, on the beach sand. This was not a great honeymoon!

Tired, sad, and pregnant, I'd go to bed; *he'd* go out. Many nights I would cry myself to sleep, repeating words that I remembered my mother saying as she would carefully apply her lipstick: "Fake it till you make it."

Many more nights I'd calm myself knowing that our baby could sense everything that I was experiencing, and so I'd softly sing lullabies until I fell asleep.

March Break

I kept working at my job as a bank teller, and I earned one week of paid vacation time. *He* finally got a job at a local mine, but *he* hadn't earned any paid vacation time yet.

I knew the baby would be born in August, so I considered taking a week to visit my family in Kipming. I'd have to take a bus there, as *he* needed the car to get to work. *He* always got to use the car.

I'd also have to take *his* little sister to visit their grandparents while I was in Kipming. I was still *his* hostage; *his* sister was *his* guarantee of my return.

I was thrilled to spend time with my family; they meant even more to me, as my secret was keeping them, this baby, and me alive.

I began a habit of painting a fake smile on my face with my lipstick, and my mother's mantra soon became mine. To keep us all alive, I also chose to fake it till I made it.

That week was heavenly … I could sleep, undisturbed, whenever I was tired. I wasn't inhaling harsh cigarette smoke or alcohol from his foul breath.

Going to church was, and still is, important to my dad. I joined them that Sunday morning. It was the first time I'd stepped back into that church since our wedding there. It felt like this was all a dream. Guilt ran coursing through my veins while I remembered the lie I'd told the priest. In my mind, I always argued with my conscience that I had to do this so *he* wouldn't kill us all.

I felt flush with this rush of emotions, and then I sensed suspicious eyes through smiling faces examining me. The familiar faces of people in the small community who supported me in all my endeavors through high school—sports, student council treasurer and then vice president, public speaking contest winner, and the town's carnival queen. I also worked after school and on weekends at one of the town's grocery stores all through high school to save money for university.

I was now beginning to look pregnant, and I was well aware that my face looked fuller too. Even though we had only been married just over one month, I was now beginning my fourth month of pregnancy. It seemed like my belly popped overnight. I could sense what they, the people in the congregation, were thinking.

I marveled at the miracle that was growing inside of me, and I poured all my love into this baby, constantly reminding myself that God must have a plan for us. That I would get pregnant from that horrible event? God must have a plan. Whenever I felt like escaping this mysterious, hellish movie of my life, I would silently repeat a prayer that my mother taught me when I was a young girl: "God grant me the serenity to accept the things I cannot change, the courage to change the things I can and the wisdom to know the difference."

Big mistake. I'd made a mistake believing that I was being courageous by staying with him under his terms because doing so was keeping me and my loved ones alive.

I was too afraid to seek advice from anyone; therefore, I lacked the wisdom to know the difference.

I often wondered if everyone's marriage was like this. Maybe everyone adapted to conditions in their households and remained quiet about the secrets that they kept in order to keep the peace or, as in my case, to stay alive.

Two more expressions that my mother would repeat also kept me alive during tumultuous times: "A still tongue is a wise head," and "I'm a lover, not a fighter."

I love my mother so much, and as I grew into a teenager, I began to call her Fred. I called her this because she was more than just my mother; she was (and still is) my *best friend*, and Fred sounds like friend. She loves this, and we have fun whenever we shop together. Sometimes, I hold up a dress in front of myself and say, "Hey, Fred, what do you think of this dress?"

21

We smile as heads turn when people hear the voice of Fred's reply come from a female. We are blessed to still carry on this way. Over time, she began to call me Ed, as it rhymes with Fred. She's so cute.

I wonder if she ever realized that I began to call her Fred following one of the happy memories that she shared with me about her father and how (with ten children) he would call her Fred. I believe that this made her feel special, and secretly (between the two of them), she was his favorite. Her birth name is April, an odd name and one that probably felt like a reminder for her parents that child number eight was born in April. Mom's eyes always lit up when she spoke about her dad, and she smiles with the memory of the twinkle in his tiny blue eyes. She has that too, especially when she's mischievous.

Her mother, Violette, was the harsh one, according to my father.

Mom's parents died within six months of each other when I was an infant. I only recognize them from my parents' wedding photo. I loved listening to the brief stories Mom and Dad would share about them. After a while, they weren't mentioned anymore. Mom would become sad at times, and Dad would say it's because she was homesick. Right after I was born, we (my parents, my sister, and I) moved three entire provinces away. We traveled by car from Nova Scotia to the border town of Kipming, Quebec. The thundering Ottawa River carried the booms of logs to the pulp and paper mill that was the primary source of income for families there, and it is the physical landmark that separates Ontario and Quebec.

The best part about growing up in Kipming was that we grew up speaking French and English without knowing that the languages were different. We even spoke to our pets in both languages.

In hindsight, I understand the significance of my mother's mantras and prayers. I understand now why she would cry and cut her hair short; she was cut off from her family … thousands of miles away, and decades would pass between visits with her siblings. I am grateful to have paid attention to her words, and I admire her strength and perseverance through difficult times. Her courage gave me courage as I would repeat to myself another one of her mantras: "Always make the best of a bad situation." And so I did.

I now forgive myself for:

- Not having the courage to share the truth about my situation with anyone
- Living in hell not even knowing what serenity felt like. Survival was my focus
- Choosing to accept that I could not change so many of the things that were happening all at once

PEARL OF WISDOM

Please tell your truth *sooner*! Have faith in a trusted friend or family member, the police, a counselor, a coworker, a confidant … someone who will help you and your family get to a safe place!

CHAPTER 5

═══ ❀ ═══

It's a Girl

Friday, August 13, 1982, I was relieved to leave work early in order to attend our friends' wedding reception being celebrated at a hotel in Espaverra, a small community just a few hours outside of Helzone, Ontario. Phidelopé was exceptionally excited about this event, and *he* declared *his* intent to party hard. I reminded *him* that our baby was to be born soon, and I cautioned *him* about the long drive back to Helzone should I go into labor.

I resolved to enjoy myself as much as I could too, and people expressed their concern for me and the baby when I joyfully participated in dancing, especially the bunny hop. It didn't take me long to feel tired, and I could see that *he* had already consumed too much alcohol to drive anyone anywhere, so I made the decision to stay at the hotel overnight. I was happy that *he* didn't follow me to our room, and I enjoyed a nice, relaxing bath before climbing into bed.

I was almost asleep when *he* stumbled into our room insisting that I not fall asleep. *He* wanted to have sex, right there and then. The smell of the alcohol, marijuana, and cigarette smoke on *his* breath made me gag as *he* recklessly forced himself onto and inside of me. The pain was too much, and I asked *him* to hurry up. *He* wouldn't, couldn't, and didn't. I felt weak when it was over and found my way to the bathroom to cry and put my nightgown back on. Thankfully, *he* was sound asleep when I went back to bed. I tried to sleep, but contractions soon started. Frequent trips to the bathroom disturbed *him*, and when *he* woke up, I explained to *him* what was happening. *He* begged for a few more hours of sleep before *he* would have to drive me to the hospital in Helzone. I was happy to let *him* sleep and sober up while I paced the hotel room floor.

When my mucus plug dislodged, I woke *him* up to encourage *him* to get us on the road. This was all happening a lot faster than I expected. Reluctantly, *he* did drive, and I cringed every time we hit a bump or had to go over the numerous train tracks along the way. Once we arrived in town, the contractions seemed to have slowed down a bit, so I encouraged *him* to sleep some more as I paced the living room floor in our tiny, basement apartment.

Saturday, August 14, 1982, at 10:35 p.m., the mystery was solved; our daughter, Désirée, was born. Tears of joy streamed down my face as I held her in my arms. That joy was quickly replaced with concern as I noticed how small her right hand was and how her fingers looked to be all the same length. The normalcy of the room immediately changed when the nurse took a closer look and whispered something to the doctor. He came over to examine her more closely from head to toe, as she lay close to my breast, too tired to feed. He then carried my newborn baby over to an incubator, and a swarm of new nurses and a pediatrician entered the room. The stillness was daunting, and it seemed to take forever before the pediatrician came over to explain to me what was happening. They found her father in the next room; *he* couldn't stomach watching the birth. Then the pediatrician shared his findings with us.

She was pretty unique. The fingers on her right hand were missing the last digit on each finger and were fused together. The thumb on that hand was normal. Her right wrist and hand were much smaller than her left. Her right foot was a club foot, and the big toe on her right foot was found almost within the arch of that foot. The specialists would conduct extensive testing to determine if anything internally was abnormal and if her fingers could eventually be safely separated.

Her vitality lit up in her beautiful blue eyes, and I treasured the miracle of life that I now held in my arms. What a blessing!

Within a few days, we left the hospital with reassurance that her vital organs and internal functions were fine. We were given the name of the pediatrician who would follow up with us in two years to prepare her for plastic surgery to separate her fingers and to correct her clubfoot.

What a relief! At least that's what I thought.

I now forgive myself for:

- Blaming myself and wondering what I did wrong that could have caused Désirée's deformities

PEARL OF WISDOM

We are all here on purpose *and* with a purpose, no matter how we got here.

CHAPTER 6

First Anniversary

Months of horror, abuse, and repeated rape led us to our first anniversary.

I felt as though I was living someone else's story, like this couldn't actually be my real life. I was pretending to be happy, showing the world that we were a happily married couple and convincing people that Phidelopé would soon find steady employment. *He* even began to attend Sunday Mass with Désirée, *his* family, and me. Then we would have Sunday brunch at *his* parents' place with the rest of *his* family, like normal families would do. Only our life was far from normal.

One Sunday afternoon, *his* family and I followed through on an intervention that we had planned for weeks. We gathered together in *his* parents' recreational room and carried on with pleasant conversation. When *he* poured *himself* a third drink within the hour following Sunday Mass, we nodded in agreement that this was the perfect time to talk to Phidelopé about *his* alcohol abuse. We filled our conversation with loving words of support for *him* and gentle persuasion for *him* to accept help and maybe even participate in an Alcoholics Anonymous program.

He loudly protested our sincere concern for *him* and chose to drink even more that afternoon until *his* father forbade *him* to have anymore. We stayed at *his* family's home the whole afternoon. *His* sisters, *his* mother, and I retreated to the kitchen to avoid *his* hostility and to prepare a hearty supper. We discussed our hopes that *he* may consider AA once *his* feelings of being ambushed would simmer down and the effects of *his* overconsumption of alcohol would wear off. It seemed to have worked. Phidelopé was civil during our meal together, and *he* did not drink anymore during or after the meal. What a relief.

Our ride home, in the early darkness that winter evenings bring, was the perfect opportunity for *him* to express *his* anger. After all, we were all strapped into our seatbelts, and *he* could get as loud as *he* wanted without anyone hearing *his* outburst. I could also not leave the vehicle that *he* was now propelling through the winding streets of Helzone, Ontario. *His* foot pressed harder on the gas pedal as *his* anger and volume increased. Désirée began to cry, and I begged *him* to slow down. This enraged *him* even more, and *he* lunged angrily toward me.

I instinctively ducked my head down as *his* fist swished past me. The windshield on my side of the car cracked and created a spiderweb pattern in the glass when *his* fist hit it instead of my head. I thought for sure we were going to have a car accident. Adrenaline pulsed through my veins, and I focused my energy on quieting our daughter as she screamed in fear. It seemed to take forever to get home.

His rant changed from anger over the intervention to blaming me for the cracked windshield. *He* went on and on about how I was going to pay for the damage. When I begged him, "Please just *stop*," *he* exploded with even more rage. In a heartbeat, *he* punched the windshield on *his* side and the webbed glass there now made it impossible for *him* to see clearly through the windshield. *His* brilliant solution was to drive with *his* window open for the rest of the way home. I knew better than to complain about the freezing-cold air that was taking our daughter's breath away. Instead, I unbuckled myself and crawled over my seat to join her in the back seat and shielded her with an extra blanket. It was a miracle that the damaged windshield did not implode. I am grateful *that* prayer was answered.

When we arrived home, Phidelopé rolled a joint; one that *he* loaded with marijuana, a chunk of something brownish-green, and a crushed white pill. I retreated to our bedroom, tucked a blanket along the bottom of the door to prevent the stench from entering the room, and lulled Désirée to sleep. Singing to her also calmed my nerves, and once she fell asleep, I gently placed her in her crib, got into my flannelette pajamas, and pulled the blankets over my head as I silently cried myself to sleep through prayers that *he* would not join me that night. *He* didn't. Thank God!

Phidelopé's stoned stupor brought *him* vivid dreams, and the next morning *he* had an announcement. Without an apology for *his* behavior from the night before, or any indication of how we would be able to afford the shattered car windshield, *his* focus was now on the next plan ...

The first anniversary gift that *he* wanted me to give *him* was to have *his* son. The memory of the previous night's horrific ordeal was still fresh in my mind. Through prayers and bargaining with my life, I thought that perhaps having a perfect son would make *him* happy enough to get a good-paying job that would support a potentially growing family, to stop indulging in alcohol and drugs, to stop dealing drugs, and to stop abusing me mentally, emotionally, physically, and sexually, effectively crushing my spirit. Then, we just might have a normal life. Wow, was I wrong!

I now forgive myself for:

- Pretending everything was "normal"

PEARL OF WISDOM

We cannot change other people.

CHAPTER 7

Twenty Years in Two

Whenever any memories of the deceptive, demented, destructive, dangerous decisions that *he* deliberately drowned us in—that Désirée and I endured throughout the twenty-two months of living hell with *the devil himself*—swirl to the surface of my memory bank and replay in my mind, I fumble through flashbacks and feelings of overwhelming shame, embarrassment, guilt, disgust, and heartfelt pain.

Flashbacks such as these: The time *he* squeezed Désirée's deformed right hand so tightly that she opened her mouth to scream from the shock and pain. Her tear-filled eyes looked at *him* in disbelief that *he* was purposely hurting her, emphasizing her imperfection, only to shove a spoonful of hot soup into her mouth. *He* did this to punish both of us—me because I asked *him* to feed her while I tidied up the food-prep area, and Désirée because she wasn't opening her mouth. She turned her head away as she felt the heat of the soup every time *he* brought it close to her face. *He* didn't put an ice cube in it to cool it down rapidly like I reminded *him* to, and *he* didn't blow on it to cool down the hot spoonful of nutritious, homemade soup that I had lovingly prepared for us to enjoy. *He* was mad about this request, as it delayed *him* from *his* plans to go golfing, and *he* had to "make some stops along the way" on *his* path to the golf course.

It all happened in seconds; yet, it's another emotional scar that haunts me still. The shrill of her scream and the sight of her beet-red, tear-streaked face and blue fingertips poking through from his big-bully grip on her tiny wrist and hand plunged me into mommy mode as I rushed to her rescue. I released her from the highchair and *his* clutching hand, and I soothed her with reassuring whispers. "I'm so sorry, sweetie … Mommy's here now … It's okay. It's okay … Shhhh, my darling … Mommy loves you."

I darted a look of disgust and disbelief toward *him*, and *he* leered back at me with a smirk of satisfaction on *his* face. Then *he* left to get on with *his* plans for the day.

My heart sank to my stomach when I noticed that the palate of Désirée's mouth was covered with a huge burn blister! Suckling on my breast would surely be painful, so I gently expressed some breast milk over her mouth and she slowly licked her lips to bring it in. The shock of this disgusting, deliberate attack exhausted both of us, and we soon fell asleep for an afternoon nap while *the monster* was away.

Sometimes Phidelopé would get excited about frightening me, especially when I would have to squash my screams of fright. *He* would hide under our bed in the bedroom that we shared with Désirée as she slept in her crib next to my side of the bed. *He* hid there as I washed up for bed, but first *he* would unscrew the light bulb of the bedroom light, unplug the lamps on the bedside tables, and draw the curtains closed so tightly that no moonlight would stream into our room. I was forced to blindly make my way to my side of the bed, farthest from the doorway. As I fumbled through the darkness and reached for the bed frame to safely guide me to my side of the bed, *he* would grasp my ankles and giggle like a little boy. Meanwhile, I was feeling frightened to death and forced myself not to scream so I wouldn't wake up our sleeping angel. *He* would repeat this until I safely jumped into our bed, frustrated, fear-filled, and confused about how this malicious ritual could bring *him* so much pleasure—so much so that when *he* would slink out from beneath the bed and lie flat on *his* back, like the king of *his* castle, *he* would have an erection.

How sick is that? I would think to myself. Anger boiled inside of me, and disgust for this human being lying next to me grew stronger each day.

He would force himself on top of me just as I was drifting off to sleep. I would quietly moan, "No, no, *no*," and plead with him to not wake up the baby. "Not now please. Tomorrow, okay?" I'd ask. But it would only arouse *him* more. Repetitious *rape* was another secret I had to keep and another insult to my self-worth … *because I didn't tell*. Once again, I wondered if that was just a part of marriage and if other women had such secrets—if the Catholic vow of marriage meant that this was just part of obeying my husband.

Sometimes, when I would glance over at *his* naked body next to me during the night while I was breastfeeding our daughter, I would be amazed at the shockingly polar opposite emotions that moved through me. As I gazed lovingly into the bluest, most beautiful eyes of my miracle marvel suckling with coos of delight, my heart would lift with overwhelming love, joy, and fulfillment. Then, while I changed her diaper, I could see *his* erection as *he* lay there, completely unaware of us, overbearingly confident—even in his sleep. I could feel my emotions sink from glee to gunk, and horrible thoughts of cutting off *his* penis and shoving it into *his* mouth (like *he* would do to me) would vividly run through my mind. I was shocked that I could have such thoughts, and I would pray for forgiveness for having them. I prayed for a better way to rid *him* from our lives, and I prayed to God for help to stop me from thinking those thoughts. I feared that I would become sick like *he* was.

The time that my parents came to visit and I excused myself from the table to breastfeed Désirée in the privacy of our bedroom situated right next to the kitchen was most frightening. Within moments of my departure from the kitchen, *he* entered the bedroom, lay on the bed next to me, and turned our world upside down with *his* disgusting question: "I wonder what it would feel like if she sucked on my cock?"

In shock, I shouted, "F—— off!"

I don't often swear, and this alarmed my parents so much that they rushed into the bedroom to see what had upset me so much. In a heartbeat, *he* jumped off the bed and lunged at my father. My mother and I, frozen in fear, watched as they punched and pushed each other right through the closet doors. My heart sank as Phidelopé's hands found the rifle that *he* stored in the closet. I really thought *he* was going to kill my dad as *he* stood over him, proudly pointing the gun at him and demanding that he and my mother mind their own business and insisting that they stay out of our lives forever. Desperation overcame me as I pleaded with *him* to put the gun down so they could pack up, and I promised to never see or speak to them again as I bargained with *him* to let them leave quietly.

They whispered pleas to me as they gathered their things, begging for Désirée and me to please leave with them. *Because I didn't tell* them of the consequences that *he* promised to fulfill if I should ever leave him, I whispered back to them with all the convincing confidence that I could put into words that I had a plan to leave, but it would have to wait.

Wow. Once again, I lied to my parents to keep us alive. The first time was when I told them that I was in love with *him* and that the literal shotgun wedding that we had planned was something we both wanted. I had then told the same lie to our priest. I would never lie before, but the fear of telling anyone the truth—that *he* would kill all of us—and my belief that *he* would led me to become a liar. Just *because I didn't tell*, right from the first time that Phidelopé raped me.

I felt like I had already lived twenty years in those incredibly miserable two years with *him*.

Someday, I would rise above *his* ego-based fear tactics. I would find the necessary courage and determination to leave. I would create a better future for us that would turn our lives right-side up and free from *his* death-grip and mental manipulation of me through *fear*!

I now forgive myself for:

- Believing *his* threats
- Not telling anyone about *his* violent temper, *his* mistreatment of Desirée and me, and *his* drug and alcohol addictions
- Enduring *his* abusive behavior
- Staying in a dangerous situation

PEARL OF WISDOM

My fear gave *him* power over me. Don't let this happen to you. Don't give your power away!

CHAPTER 8

❋

Another Child

Life with *him* was so horrific, unpredictable, physically unbearable, and emotionally draining that I found myself imagining that this life was someone else's story. I sacrificed my own self-worth, dignity, integrity, and peace of mind in order to keep the peace. I lived in constant fear of *his* reaction to anything that *he* disagreed with. Phidelopé's anger was off the charts, and *he* would lash out with harsh words and violent reactions.

His disapproval of our daughter's physical imperfection was clear, and I was always watchful of *his* interaction with her, especially when *he* would purposefully squeeze her deformed right hand. The incident that I had witnessed was blurred by the new suspicion that I had: that *he* might be abusing her sexually. I would purposely block these thoughts out, telling myself that *he* must be satisfied with the constant sexual abuse that *he* continuously put me through.

Those fears were amplified the morning that I awoke to hear Désirée screaming over the sound of *his* laughter and coaxing her that she was okay. I rushed toward the sound of running water, and when I flung open the shower curtain, I was shocked to see that *he* was sporting another erection, and poor Désirée was hovering just above it. Horrified, I grabbed our daughter from *his* odd grip on her, and

I held her close to my heart as I wrapped her in her towel and ran to our room to console and dress her. I was shaking with disbelief at what I had just witnessed, and I checked her for damage. I couldn't even imagine what that would look like, and I inhaled deeply as I put a fresh diaper on her. It looked like she may be starting a diaper rash, and I was too confused and overwhelmed with fear to think otherwise.

We never spoke about what happened that morning, and I *never* allowed *him* to have a bath or a shower with her again.

Days turned into weeks, and weeks turned into months. One day, as I was mentally rehashing the horror of *his* mistreatment of *his* own infant daughter, I wondered how *he* would ever see past her imperfection and focus on her heaven-sent beauty and wonderful behavior. Surprisingly, the thought of having *his* son was the answer that popped into my head. I remembered that this was the gift that *he* wanted for our first anniversary. Phidelopé really wanted a son—one more thing that our daughter was not. The more I thought about this, the greater relief I felt with regard to my quest to distract *him* from inflicting more abuse upon our innocent daughter and me.

My intelligent self argued with my frightened self about how ridiculous this idea was. I prayed for a better solution; however, in my overwhelmingly frightened and emotionally unstable state, I could not imagine a different solution. Always, there was the idea of leaving *him*, and always, that idea was banished with visions of my dead family—the follow-through of the threat that *he* regularly reminded me of if I should ever leave *him*.

He, the sex addict, was quite excited with the idea of creating a son. I stopped taking birth control pills, and it wasn't long before I announced to Phidelopé and our families that we were going to have another baby. *He* was over-the-moon excited, and I was suddenly faced with the fact that there was no guarantee that this baby was a boy. I vowed to love this child no matter what the gender, and I chose to be grateful that my body welcomed another fetus. I prayed wholeheartedly for a healthy child and for God to "Please bless us with a son."

Needless to say, my parents were mortified with the news.

I now forgive myself for:

- Being foolish enough to believe that another child would make *him* a better person
- Putting the people I love through so much turmoil

PEARL OF WISDOM

Children are *miracles*! Please, everyone, treat them as such.

CHAPTER 9

Cheater!

Throughout this contract called marriage, I was met with numerous indicators that Phidelopé was a cheater. *He* was often unemployed; yet, numerous times *he* would be away from home for entire days and late into the evening. When *he* did come home, *he* smelled of alcohol, cigarettes, marijuana, and sweat. *He* never told me where *he* was going, and *he* didn't call while *he* was away. Honestly, I enjoyed the quiet and joyful time spent alone with our daughter. During one of those peaceful days, I received a phone call from a young lady. I remember her youthful, excitedly nervous voice as she spoke, "Hello. Can I speak to Phidelopé please?"

I remembered being polite in my response. "No, I'm sorry, *he's* not here right now. May I take a message for *him*?"

I guess she thought I was *his* mother, because she giggled girlishly with her response. "Well, I think I left my gloves in *his* car. Will you please let *him* know?"

My heart sank, and I felt weirdly warm as the realization of *his* infidelity rang through my ears and numbed me for a moment. I told her I would definitely get that message to *him*. I also boldly announced to her that I was *his* pregnant wife, and I firmly advised her that she should find a single man to drive around with.

I remember feeling my heart pounding in my chest, and I felt sick to my stomach with the realization that this could be the reason for the numerous yeast infections that I had been experiencing since being with *him*.

The sound of my daughter's babbling as she amused herself with books and toys in her playpen brought me back to reality.

I pondered this strange reality and questioned myself:

Why do I stay?

Will he really kill our children, my family members, and me if I do leave?

What have I done?

Why am I struggling with my religious belief in the sacred vow of marriage when he is obviously not?

Why am I so afraid to tell?

Ashamed and afraid, I looked at my beautiful daughter, gently spoke to her and my unborn child about how much I love them, and, like a robot, I chose to make the best of this horrible mess and always be the best mom that I could be.

Many nights that followed I refused to let *him* touch me, and I remember thinking those horrible thoughts again about how I'd like to cut off *his* always-erect penis while *he* slept next to me and shove it into *his* mouth. I would pray that this would kill *him,* and then I could escape with one child in my arms and pregnant with another.

These thoughts would shock me, as this was clearly not like me. I was afraid of whom I was becoming.

Overwhelmed with repeated events of sexual, physical, and verbal abuse, as well as the emotional despair I felt and my fear of contracting a sexually transmitted disease from *his* promiscuity and infidelity, I found myself desperately thinking of ways to escape this nightmare of a life. Always, Phidelopé's threats would keep me there. I didn't want to be the reason my children, parents, and siblings would die. I was already dead inside. Thankfully, the love for my darling toddler and unborn child kept me alive and determined to keep them happy, healthy, and safe from the monster of a man they had to call Dad.

I now forgive myself for:

- Staying with him

PEARL OF WISDOM

Marriage is to be respected, as are the people who commit to it. Love, honor, and *respect* each other.

CHAPTER 10

The Card

I was taking Désirée for a walk in her stroller when I noticed a law office across from the city courthouse. I figured I must have walked past it at least a hundred times before. On this day, I stopped outside the office, parked the stroller, picked up my precious baby, and found myself in the lawyer's office. I vividly remember the intense grip of fear—fear that *he* was watching me, fear that *he'd* burst into the office at any time. I still don't remember the steps I took to get me inside the lawyer's office.

The sound of the receptionist's voice echoed in my ears and slowly brought me back to reality as she asked, "How may I help you?"

I remember looking around and feeling relief that no one else was there.

I whispered, "How do I get a divorce, and how much will it cost?"

She answered with a question that stunned me, "How long have you been legally separated?"

In shock, I replied, "We're not separated. I just need a divorce!"

She went on to explain that we must be legally separated for six consecutive months in order to apply for a divorce. My heart sank, and it felt like I had been there for much too long already. I was so afraid that *he* might drive by and recognize the stroller parked outside the law office.

She asked one more question as I asked for and quickly grabbed the lawyer's business card and tucked it inside my bra.

"Is there abuse? Are you being abused?"

"Yes," I answered, and I quickly headed out the door, holding my precious baby girl close to my heart, and her unborn sibling flip-flopped within my womb. As the door was closing behind me, the secretary asked one more question: "Is your child being abused?"

The door closed. The answer was still my secret.

I rushed home and hid that business card in a secret compartment in my wallet. I prayed *he* would never find it.

I now forgive myself for:

- Not answering the receptionist's question
- Leaving the office without setting an appointment to speak with the lawyer

PEARL OF WISDOM

When opportunities present themselves to you, do everything you can to make the best of them, for your good and the highest good of all.

CHAPTER 11

❀

Mémère Upstairs

I did my best to feel at home in our tiny one-bedroom basement apartment. I kept it exceptionally clean, neat, and tidy. I would even scrub the kitchen floor on my hands and knees, and I would wax it that way too. Whenever we had guests over, they would remark on how shiny the kitchen floor was. In hindsight, my obsession with cleaning was a cover-up for the real mess—the life that I was living.

I enjoyed spending time upstairs with our landlady. She told us to just call her Mémère like everyone else did. She was a kind and loving lady who was raising her teenage grandson. Her face would light up whenever Désirée and I would visit her. She spoke fondly of her husband who had passed away years ago and shared her concerns for her grandson, as he was quickly growing into a young man and wasn't showing any ambition. Often, late in the evening, I would hear him arguing with her, and then the door upstairs would slam shut as he would leave, still muttering insults to her. Then I would hear her pacing the living room floor, praying and crying. I felt so bad for her. I had little respect for him, and I chose to ignore him.

For a brief while, I noticed that Mémère was away. The next time I saw her grandson I couldn't ignore him. I asked him if everything was okay and questioned where his grandmother had been lately.

I could smell alcohol on his breath as he slurred an answer. "She's in the hospital. They're trying to figure out what's wrong with her."

That was all he said before entering their home and closing the door. I wanted to know more. Which hospital? What room? Was she allowed to have visitors?

I thought it was so kind of Phidelopé to run upstairs to see her grandson when I explained to *him* my concerns for Mémère. What a fool I was. This was just a perfect opportunity for the two of them to smoke cigarettes and marijuana and drink alcohol. I didn't wait up for *him* that night. I was too furious about *his* immaturity and their total lack of respect for Mémère.

I heard the grandson stumble into the house one evening, and then I could hear him moving around in the kitchen. He was dropping things on the kitchen floor and then cranked up the music. I covered my ears with my pillow and tried to go back to sleep.

Later, my incessant coughing woke me up. When I looked around, I could see that our room was filled with smoke. Something was on fire! Alarmed, I quickly picked up our sleeping baby and shook Phidelopé awake. *He* was very angry about being woken up that way. I insisted that we needed to get out of the apartment as quickly as possible. I immediately dialed 911 for the fire department, and *he* ran upstairs to check on the grandson. While I bundled up our baby and climbed the sixteen stairs to our exit, I could hear the grandson coughing and gasping for air.

Once he was pulled outside to safety, I asked him what had happened. He figured that he had passed out while cooking something to eat, and it all caught on fire—the food, the pan, and the stove. As relieved as I was to see him alive, I was equally as infuriated about his irresponsibility and his total lack of respect for Mémère, her home, and us. The kitchen was damaged by the fire and water, and thankfully, the rest of the house, including our apartment, only sustained smoke damage. We stayed at Phidelopé's parents' place during the renovation upstairs and while the smoke smell lifted from our tiny apartment.

When we returned, I was relieved to see that Mémère was home too. She looked frail and had lost some weight. That evening, I went upstairs to see how she was feeling. She shared with me her diagnosis of cancer. In the months that followed, her deterioration was rapid. My days were busier now chasing a toddler and preparing for the arrival of our next baby. Whenever *he* was sober and home for an evening, I would ask Phidelopé to listen for our sleeping daughter while I would go upstairs to rub lotion on Mémère's aching back and swollen feet. We grew quite close, and I looked forward to our visits together as much as she did.

She died in her sleep one miserable March night, and in the morning when we got the news of her death, I began spotting blood. Oh no! Was this baby going to die too? My doctor ordered complete bed rest for the rest of this pregnancy. I was sad to be unable to attend Mémère's funeral yet very relieved to still have a baby's heart beating within my womb.

It was impossible to maintain complete bed rest with a curious toddler on the move and no one around to help me. Phidelopé would disappear for hours each day looking for a job, or so *he'd* say. My family lived three and a half hours away, and my siblings and father worked full time. Mom didn't know how to drive. *His* family lived in town; yet, they also worked, and *his* mother would only take care of Désirée if I went to their house with her. Whenever *he* was around, I had to always beg for *his* assistance with the housework and some of the chores to keep our apartment clean and tidy.

Phidelopé became infuriated with my request for *him* to wash the kitchen floor while I took a much-needed rest, and *he* spat in my face. *He* then yelled, "No! You're just pregnant! You're not crippled! Do it yourself!"

With that, *he* stormed out the door. This was truly a new level of *low*. It was pure hell living with *him*. I pulled that card out of my wallet and began to dial the lawyer's office when … *thump, thump, thump, thump, thump* … *Oh no!* I thought. *He* was coming down the stairs! I quickly tucked the card into my bra and hung up the phone. I pretended to be reading a book while rocking our baby when *he* rushed right passed us to pick up *his* wallet. *He* left in a hurry without even saying good-bye. Intense fear and extreme fatigue kept me from dialing that number again.

I now forgive myself for:

- Not speaking to Mémère's children about her grandson's behavior
- Enduring more abuse and insults
- Allowing fear to interfere with my common sense
- Not following through with the call to the lawyer at that time
- Not choosing to go live with my parents and never return after the fire

PEARL OF WISDOM

We are all born with unconditional love. It's the circumstances of life and how we choose to handle those circumstances that create the conditions of life that we are experiencing. Therefore, choose wisely.

CHAPTER 12

Alone

June 12, 1984, I was enjoying my stroll to the doctor's office for my weekly appointment, as baby number two was due. I was also relieved that my firstborn child had been with my parents for the past few days so I could rest up and prepare properly for the heightened level of responsibility that soon would be upon me—the experience of being home with two little children under the age of two.

Upon examination, the doctor explained that I had begun to dilate, and I was at four centimeters. He advised me to go home, grab my suitcase, and get to the hospital. He was confident that I would deliver my baby that day.

I was excited and worried at the same time. The walk home was all uphill, and I had no idea where Phidelopé was at the time.

My hospital bag had been packed for the past few months, as this pregnancy was filled with all kinds of surprises: premature contractions, blood show, increased frequency and duration of migraines, and extreme fatigue. Experiencing all of this while taking care of another child was very stressful; the prescribed complete bed rest never happened. *He* was rarely home, and even when *he* was, *he* didn't help. I was too afraid to question *his* routine. I only knew that *he* wasn't working, and our only income was *his* meager unemployment benefit cheque.

I did a quick check around the house to make sure everything would be ready for my return from the hospital, and then I called *his* mother to take me to the hospital. She asked if I wanted her to stay with me, and I expressed, with grave concern, that the most important thing to do was to find her son.

The experience of spending hours *alone* in the labor room was actually comforting to me. I focused on myself, on gentle breathing, and on loving this baby all the way through to delivery. Down the hall there were screams of agony and panic happening as other women were bringing their children into the world. I meditated with intent to block out all of that. I focused on controlled breathing and the miraculous birthing process.

By 1:30 that afternoon I was fully dilated, and I soon felt the urge to push. They rushed me into the delivery room, and at 2:31 on that sunny Tuesday afternoon, my beautiful second daughter was born. I counted all of her fingers and her toes while paying special attention to confirm that they were normal.

"Yes!" I whispered in delight.

This child had no obvious abnormalities. I was so grateful. When they placed her warm body on top of mine, she immediately urinated. She certainly showed me how alive she was. Then I felt gruelling pressure on my tummy as the delivery nurse pressed down with force on it to encourage the placenta to be released. A weird and uncomfortable feeling came over me; something was different. As the placenta was delivered, I heard myself say out loud, "That was not just a placenta!"

The entire room and the energy in it changed. They placed my daughter to my breast to encourage her to feed and to distract me while specialists entered the room to examine the placenta. I knew then that this was not just the placenta. It was another baby!

They began asking me questions about twins in the family.

"Yes," I told them. "There are twins on *his* side of the family."

Excitedly, I shared with them that I always wanted to have twins. This was quite a surprise.

The silence in the room and the busyness around this child worried me. Intuitively, I knew that the child was not alive. I asked them if it was a boy. A nurse slowly turned around to face me and sadly nodded her head, indicating a yes.

One of the obstetricians came over and asked me if I had plans for the child. I was stunned for a moment, overwhelmed with the elation of having a son—the twins that I so desired. Then, in an instant, I felt deep sorrow as I realized that I would not be taking our son home.

Our home environment, and my life, was so filled with violence on every level: mental, emotional, physical, and sexual. I knew it was toxic for me and now my two girls. I had already planned to leave Phidelopé after this baby was born. I remembered the lawyer's business card that I had picked up on one of my walks with Desirée. That was going to be my ticket *out*.

With the best interest for my two children and myself in my mind, I pondered the decision that I had to make without *him*. I really did not have the chance to grow attached to this third child, as I didn't even know that he had existed until he was born. Ultrasound technology was new at that time and only utilized for emergency situations. I instructed the specialist to keep our son for the benefit of research and science. If he could help them, and any other parents of children in this situation, his death would serve a great purpose. I named him Daxon.

I vowed then, and pleaded with the entire team in the room with me, to never, ever reveal this to Daxon's father. I knew in my heart and the very core of my being that something horrible would happen to me if Phidelopé ever found out that *he* had a son who didn't survive. Thankfully, the entire team agreed to keep Daxon a secret.

The shock and grief of delivering and losing Daxon was quickly soothed with the joy and love that filled my heart as I held my seven-pound, one-ounce daughter in my arms. We looked at each other as she, Victoria, nursed, and I believe we intuitively shared this secret about her twin brother and would carry it with us for the rest of our lives. I knew she was strong, and I felt very grateful for that.

The journey ahead would be challenging, and I prayed for assistance, courage, patience, and perseverance. I was grateful for Daxon having chosen to surrender his time with us, almost as though he knew that what lay ahead for me and his two sisters would not be pleasant. It would be much easier with two children under the age of two rather than three.

I now forgive myself for:

- Not insisting to have an ultrasound when I was spotting; that's probably when Daxon failed to thrive
- Putting the twins through such stress—it must have felt as hot as hell in that womb

51

PEARL OF WISDOM

You can choose to do one of two things during a time of crisis. You can pray, *or* you can worry. To worry when you pray sends a message out to the heavenly helpers that you don't believe that your prayers are being heard. *Pray with faith* that your prayers are heard, and you will receive divine guidance. Worry is not productive, and it will only serve to wear you down.

CHAPTER 13

Seriously?

My parents packed up twenty-two-month-old Désirée and began the drive to Helzone the moment that I called them to let them know I was going to the hospital to deliver her sister or brother. I was happy to be reunited with our firstborn later that afternoon, and it was amazing to see how grown-up she looked sitting next to me while I was holding her new little sister, Victoria. My parents took a picture of us: me, Désirée, and Victoria, sitting there in the lobby before they left the hospital that afternoon. Then they went to our apartment with Désirée and waited for *him* to show up. Amazingly, Phidelopé was still nowhere to be found.

From time to time, I pull out this photo from our photo album, and every time I look at it, tears begin to well up in my eyes. I stare at little Désirée's happy, smiling face, and I gaze into her innocent, beautiful blue eyes, and I realize that her life—all of our lives—were forever changed when *he,* her father, finally did show up that evening.

The awkward silence and the bewildered expression that I saw on my parents' faces upon my arrival to our tiny basement apartment the next morning told me that something must have happened. I pretended that everything was okay, and I encouraged Phidelopé to go to the grocery store to pick up some necessities and groceries so I could prepare a nice meal for all of us. *He* reluctantly agreed to this and stomped up the stairs and slammed the door as *he* stepped out.

Once I settled our newborn, Victoria, into her cradle and placed Désirée into the playpen, my parents whispered, wide-eyed and horrified, about the dramatic, life-changing events that they had witnessed and overheard the previous night. Through tears and gasping for breath, they shared the following story with me:

Phidelopé was very excited to see Désirée, and *he* fussed over her that evening with a childlike enthusiasm, much like a child getting a new puppy. *He* played with her and hardly acknowledged them except during supper when *he* thanked my mom for preparing the meal for them. It wasn't long after supper that *he* scooped up little Désirée and said *he* was going to put her to bed. *He* dismissed himself by stating that it was a big day for everyone, and she must be tired—*he* was too. *He* told them not to worry if they were to hear Désirée crying.

"She does that to fight her sleep," *he* said, and *he* warned them not to enter the bedroom no matter what they heard.

They said they heard laughter at first. They could tell *he* was tickling her because they could hear *him* also laughing as *he* repeated, "Tickle, tickle, tickle."

Then the crying began. They said they were concerned, but they remembered *his* warning, and vivid visions of the last scuffle in that room with the gun in the closet kept them from entering. Through tears, they recounted how they prayed together to calm themselves from entering the bedroom, especially when the tearful screams from little Désirée sounded more frightening. They said they could hear *him* shushing her by pleading, "It's okay. You're okay."

After a while, they said it was very quiet. They figured that Phidelopé must have fallen asleep because *he* never came out of the room that night until the alarm woke him up the next morning. Désirée stayed quiet all that time too.

With a shudder, my mother went on to explain the horror that she saw when she checked to see why Désirée was screaming when she sat on the potty for her morning pee-pee. She first noticed a scratch on Désirée's forehead and recalls wondering how that could have happened. When she lifted Désirée from the potty and held her close to console her and wipe her private area, she was alarmed to notice a bruise on Désirée's inner thigh of her right leg. Reluctantly, she brought this to the attention of my father, and together they carefully examined her and gasped when they saw her raw, torn, and bruised vulva as they laid her on the change table to put a fresh diaper on her.

We all did our best to maintain some sense of composure during this nightmare of a conversation for the sake of little Désirée who was quietly playing in her playpen as new baby Victoria was sleeping peacefully in her cradle in the very room that was wrought with the disturbing activity the night before. I remember slumping onto a kitchen chair as the details of this most horrific event swirled through my head. Mom and Dad sat too, apologizing profusely for not stepping in and being too nervous about entering the room the night before. Their feelings of guilt were palpable. Then, my father's protective instinct set in, and he expressed the urgent need for all of us to leave—*now*—while Phidelopé was out getting groceries. They began to collect their suitcases and proceeded up the sixteen stairs only to pause in bewilderment about my hesitation to follow them. My father settled my mother into their vehicle and placed the suitcases in the trunk, and with the motor running, he rushed back into our kitchen, begging me once more to hurry up and leave with them. Through tears, I declined their offer for our safety. *His* promise—*his* threat—to kill everyone whom I would tell this shameful, horrible truth to still haunted me. I did *not* want to be responsible for that too!

I pleaded. "Dad, I promise you I will leave, just not right now. Believe me, we cannot do this right now! Please, please trust and know that I will keep myself and these baby girls safe. There's just one important thing that I need to do first."

I promised him that I would call the police, and with that assurance, my dad reluctantly climbed the sixteen stairs to daylight. With a heavy heart and tears streaming down his face, he said, "See you soon, Itzabella. Be careful. I hope you know what you're doing."

I nodded to him and wiped my own tears before picking up little Désirée and rocking her to sleep through tearful lullabies.

I prayed for calmness and courage to face Phidelopé upon *his* return. Thankfully, I was blessed with both.

He was not upset to see that my parents had departed, and *he* sat down while I quietly put the groceries away. When I asked *him* if *he* had a difficult time putting Désirée to bed the night before, *he* confidently answered, "No, not at all."

When I questioned *him* about the scratch on her forehead, *he* said *he* may have accidently scratched her during the night because *he* didn't bother putting her in her crib once she fell asleep. *He* must have been prepared for my next questions, and I was shocked with how smoothly *he* transformed our discussion when he said, "Did you know that a girl can pop her cherry just by doing the splits?"

I stumbled to find an appropriate response to such a bizarre question. I knew this was confirmation of what *he had just done* to our daughter, and I was grateful for the immediate divine wisdom that came to me to not alarm *him* and to go along with this crazy conversation.

I took a deep breath and said, "Where did you hear such a silly thing?" I couldn't even look at *him*. I was so disgusted. I thought to myself, *What kind of a sick person does this to a child? His own child? Who does this?* I didn't need to know the depths of this answer. I knew now that we, me and my two little girls, just had to get away as soon as possible.

His answer was ridiculous. "I think I heard it on the news a while ago."

But the answer didn't really matter to me, and I slowly walked away from *him* to find my purse. I ended our conversation by saying, "Seriously?"

My mind became too busy with plans for what to do next to even acknowledge *his* presence. I was relieved when *he* said *he* had to go out again, stupidly explaining that *he* forgot to buy cigarettes.

As *his* car sped away, I quickly and carefully secured both children into the big Gendron baby carriage and rapidly walked to our family doctor's office. I didn't have an appointment, but we were immediately whisked into a private room in the busy, downtown office when I answered, "Incest," to the receptionist's question: "Why are you here today? You are not in the schedule."

Dr. Cho entered the room in record time. By the concerned look on his face, I could tell that his receptionist had informed him of the reason for our visit. He pulled a fresh section of paper over the examining table, and I began to undress Désirée to be examined by Dr. Cho. I grew to admire his professionalism throughout my pregnancies; he was the doctor whom I'd chosen for me and our growing family, and I was grateful that he did not hesitate to help us out now. He was kind and gentle with Désirée as he examined her, even though this procedure was admittedly stressful and frightening for her—for all of us. Before Dr. Cho could finish his sentence revealing his conclusion from his examination of twenty-two-month-old Désirée, Phidelopé (*the monster*) stormed into the room.

"Oh, that's just the rash she gets when she drinks too much orange juice!" *he* declared. *He* took over, quickly redressing our daughter and rushing us out of the room before anything else could be said or done.

"Seriously!" was the last word I said to *him* that day.

I knew that *he* knew what we dared not talk about!

My heart ached, and part of me died that day. The only thought that got me through the next few weeks was to find that lawyer's business card so at the first safe opportunity I had, I could make that call.

I now forgive myself for:

- Not thinking the unthinkable
- Believing that I had everything under control
- Keeping these secrets that ultimately endangered our children too

PEARL OF WISDOM

If someone hurts you once and you do nothing about it, they *will* hurt you again. *You must* save yourself. Tell someone. *Report abuse*!

CHAPTER 14

Ticket to Freedom

When my dad called and told me that my mother had herniated a spinal disc from their rushed exit from our apartment that brutal day, I knew I had to see her. I explained to Phidelopé how important it was for me to be with her as my father, sister, and brother all worked during the day and how dangerous it was for my mother to be alone all day in her incapacitated state. I was pleased when *he* agreed to let me go to be with her and not at all surprised that *he* insisted that I travel to Kipming with *his* twelve-year-old sister, Nancy, by Greyhound Bus with our two children. Once again, she was *his* guarantee of our return within the timeline and clear boundaries that *he* set for us. *His* sister would visit their grandparents, while I helped Mom out and took care of Désirée and Victoria too. I thanked *him* and promised to be home, with our children and *his* sister, on time for Victoria's baptism.

"Tickets please. May I see your tickets please?" These were the most life-changing words I had heard in a long time.

I smiled with relief as the bus driver reviewed our tickets, knowing that this was our ticket to freedom. The two-hour layover in Hapland, Ontario, was hardly an inconvenience compared to the past few years that we'd spent with *the devil himself. His* grandparents offered to drive me the extra ten miles to my parents' place when they picked up their granddaughter at the station in Kipming, Quebec, but I politely turned them down. Instead, I asked the bus driver to drop the three of us in front of my parents' home, which was on the highway that would take the remaining passengers to their Northern Quebec destinations.

I felt as though I was watching a movie as we disembarked the bus, and that is exactly what it must have looked like for anyone else who was watching. The bus driver put the four-way flashers on, put the bus in park, opened the bus door, stepped down onto the gravel in my parents' driveway entrance, and put his hand out to carefully guide me, with Victoria strapped to me in her snuggly, and little Désirée holding on to me with her tiny arms around my neck and her little legs wrapped around my waist. He tipped his hat to me in a kind and gentlemanly farewell gesture as I rolled our one suitcase toward my family home. I whispered to myself in gratitude to God for keeping us safe on our journey. "Yes, we made it! Thank God."

We were smothered with hugs and kisses from my dad as he met us at the door. I knelt down beside my mom, who was resting on the couch, too sore and weak to stand up. I placed Victoria next to her. She cried tears of joy—we all did. It was such a relief to be there.

Dad made us a wonderful meal, and the children fell asleep early that evening. The conversation that followed gave my parents much more information than any parent would want to hear. It was not my plan to tell them all the details of what I had been through; yet, the words, like a mighty river flowing, did not cease until the entire truth was revealed. My father gathered up the parade of snotty, tear-filled tissues that we had gone through as my mother and I washed up in preparation for bed. We retired that night with the agreement that I would call the lawyer, the mystery man whose card I'd hung onto and had hidden for months, first thing the next morning. Exhausted and emotionally spent, I slept better that night than I had in years.

I now forgive myself for:

- Agreeing to *his* terms
- Deceiving *his* little sister

PEARL OF WISDOM

Take your leap of faith and move forward fearlessly.

CHAPTER 15

❋

Ridiculous!

When I called the next day, the receptionist remembered me and expressed her relief that I was now in a safe place. She agreed to have the lawyer call me later that day, as I was unable to meet him in person. He was kind and very patient as he listened to the details of our lives, and he expressed that he would initiate our legal separation immediately. He reassured me that I would never have to see Phidelopé again, and he would have a messenger deliver the notice of my intent to begin the legal separation process to *him* in person the next day. Wow! I had been so frightened for so long that I had a hard time to believe that it could be so easy. What a relief!

That feeling of relief was short-lived. Upon signing for and reviewing the documents that the messenger delivered to *him*, Phidelopé immediately dialed my parents' phone number. I knew, by the look on my mother's pale face exactly who was calling when she handed me the receiver.

I took a slow deep breath and in a quivering voice I said, "Hello."

I was surprised to hear that *he* was laughing. *He* was certain someone was playing a joke on *him*.

"Who would do such a crazy thing? Who knew you were going to be away? This is a prank that I would play on one of my buddies. Who did you plan this with? It even makes it seem more real by having someone pretend to be a messenger and have me sign for it. This is so cool!" *he* rambled on.

His laughter turned into a heated hysteria when I told *him* it was not a joke.

"It's for real," I said. "You had to sign for it because it is a legal separation document, and you must take it seriously."

He immediately pulled on *his* big-bully pants, and I had to hold the receiver away from my ear as *he* viciously uttered threats until I hung up the phone. I knew I had entered another wrestling match with *him*—one that would require a lot of patience and money.

It wasn't long before I received a call from my lawyer acknowledging receipt of a letter from *his* lawyer. During our conversation, my lawyer advised me that he would not be able to pursue my case unless I had a place to live in within Ontario. I reassured him that our stay at my parents' place was only temporary. I would have an Ontario address with our new place of residence ready for him before our next scheduled phone call. He also instructed me to seek financial aid with the help from a legal aid office in Hapland, Ontario. I slumped onto the sofa following that conversation. My head was spinning.

Where am I going to live now? Will my sister and her husband want to share their apartment with their two infant nieces and me? How and when will I get to Hapland? What is legal aid, and will I qualify? Oh my God, what have I done now?

My mother's soft voice echoed in my ears. "Are you okay? Can I get you some tea?"

I held Victoria to my breast to feed, and Désirée played with her toys on the carpet in the living room as I discussed this new development with my mother. She reassured me that everything would be fine and that she and my father would help me through everything that was necessary in order to finalize this separation and keep us safe from all harm. I knew she was right; however, I also knew that I had literally poked the bear, and *he* and *his* family would not go easy on me. They had lots of money, and the lawyer they hired for *him* proved this.

My brother took a day off from work to drive me to Hapland for my appointment with legal aid. It was the first time that I ever left my two children with anyone else. I was glad that my father stayed home that day to help my mother take care of them while I was miles away taking care of a new future for us. My sister and her husband graciously made room for all three of us, and I was able to give my new Ontario address to the receptionist upon my arrival at the legal aid office. I asked her for clarity with the question about my income.

"You have to give details of the money you receive," was her reply.

I explained to her that I had zero income. I had not returned to work after giving birth to Désirée, and the maternity leave benefits that I did receive after she was born had stopped several months earlier.

To this, she bluntly said, "Well then, put down zero dollars. Your lawyer will set up alimony and child support payments for you."

I had no idea what she was talking about. I didn't know anyone who had gone through a separation. All of this was new to me.

My brother and I were greeted by a kind young lady who reviewed my forms prior to calling us into the privacy of her office. She approved my application and handed me a list of lawyers who accepted clients with legal aid. More new territory... I was ashamed of my naivety. I chose a female lawyer with hopes that she would be empathetic. A call was placed to her office by the kind lady, and she nodded in agreement as she wrote down a date for me to meet the lawyer. I was disappointed that it wasn't going to be that same day, and I shared my concern with the kind lady who was patiently taking care of me. She bowed her head and sadly explained the numerous appointments and process that I was now embarking upon and suggested that I look for a place to live in Hapland with my two daughters.

In tears, I expressed my frustration, "How am I supposed to find us an apartment with no money to even feed us?"

She kindly explained about a benefit for single parents called Mother's Allowance and told my brother where that office was located.

"While you are there," she said, "you might as well apply for public housing. There's a long list, and it may take a while before an affordable place is found for you and your two girls."

Once more, my head was spinning with new information. I was so grateful to have my brother drive me all around that day; he would make me laugh whenever he sensed that I could really burst into tears. We made great strides that day. We also remembered to pick up a Hapland newspaper on our way back to my sister's place to look for an apartment that would accept me and my two precious little girls within the immediate future.

A temporary visitation order was set in motion, and when I protested such a request, we were assigned to a social worker within the Children's Aid Society. I was grateful for the delay that this created, as it also allowed Désirée, Victoria, and me some much-needed time to settle into our new two-bedroom, second-floor, spacious apartment that I'd found in Hapland, Ontario. The cost for such a place ate up most of my first Mother's Allowance check, and I was grateful that the landlord waived the requirement of having first and last month's rent upfront. We could live there without a phone until the cheaper apartment across the street would become available within two months. I felt truly blessed!

The social worker assigned to me and Désirée was a man; this made me feel uncomfortable and nervous. He was soft-spoken, and after a while, I began to feel more comfortable.

He, with sincere empathy, explained to me why he chose to become a social worker. He gave Désirée a toy to play with and went on to say, "I know what you are going through. Nobody believed me either, not even my mother, when I told her that my uncle was sexually abusing me. I know the courage that it takes to come forward with this, and I am glad to see that you are taking a stand for your daughter. Please, now tell me what happened."

The hour with him flew by, and I continued to wipe away tears as he escorted Désirée and me out of his office. We scheduled another appointment before leaving, and he explained that Désirée would be the first child to work with sexually correct dolls in that district of Ontario. I wasn't really sure what he meant by this, and I didn't bother to ask any questions. I just wanted to take the city bus back to our apartment and put this all behind us.

I was grateful to have made friends with the kind lady who lived across the hall from us. Sharon was a stay-at-home mom, and her son was Désirée's age. Her husband, a tall, slim, yet solid man, worked each day. They always shared tender kisses and quiet good-byes in the mornings as he left. Her kind heart and love of children was sincere, and I was relieved to leave Victoria with her while Désirée and I met with the CAS counselor. October's chill seemed to penetrate my bones on our bus ride, so Désirée and I cuddled together on one seat to keep warm. A pleasant cup of tea with my neighbor when we picked up Victoria helped too. The children played well together, while Sharon and I discussed the details of the appointment. I was glad to have someone who attentively listened, and she gave me great reassurance from her knowledge of the CAS system. Her parents took care of foster children and went on to adopt a few of them as well. Before leaving her place an hour later, I thought I should give Sharon a brief description of Phidelopé ... just in case *he* would sneak around to find out where I, and his daughters, lived. She promised me that *he* would never get that information from her. I felt the sincerity in her promise, and we smiled at each other as we closed and locked our apartment doors for the night.

It wasn't long after that I fed and bathed the girls and sang them lullabies. I fed, burped, and changed Victoria. When I tucked the two girls into their crib and infant bed, I was ready for bed too. As I laid my head upon my pillow, suddenly, my creativity crept in, and ideas for Halloween costumes for the children popped into my head. It was the first time in years that happy thoughts sparked enthusiasm inside of me. I finally felt safe enough and peaceful enough to bring some normalcy into our world. I leapt out of my bed to gather materials for their costumes while they slept. I was so excited, and I realized that my time during the day was too busy chasing Victoria in her walker and Désirée around the kitchen and living room areas and down the hallway to our bedrooms during their waking hours, so I acted quickly and quietly.

Victoria's was an easy ensemble; she would be a young Elton John. I poked the lenses out of a pair of her sunglasses and wrapped the frames with tinfoil. She had very little, very fair hair, and any sleeper would do for a five-and-a-half-month-old to wheel around in while in her walker among the three other neighbors' apartments on our floor. Désirée was going to be Little Red Riding Hood. The red fall coat with matching hat that someone donated to us was a perfect fit and the best costume for my precious two-year-old. I fell asleep, happy and grateful that night. Ahhhhh!

The next morning I got up early to take the girls grocery shopping and to get some Halloween treats to dish out as well. I scurried into our apartment in a state of frenzy because I thought I caught a glimpse of Phidelopé's car pulling into our parking lot as I was dragging the heavy stroller over the final step up into our apartment building's rear entranceway. God gave me wings and strength because I still don't remember how I got the kids, the groceries, the stroller, and myself up the stairs and into our apartment and safely closed and locked the apartment door just in time to hear the main floor door (no security lock in those days) of the apartment's rear entranceway swing open.

I hushed the girls and quickly moved them to their back bedroom and gave them toys to play with in the playpen while I snuck up to my door, made sure the bolt lock was in lock position, and squeamishly peered through the peephole. I held my breath as *he* knocked on the three apartment doors of the first level. I wasn't even sure it was Phidelopé, but the terror I felt was all too familiar. I double-checked the locks as *his* footsteps were now climbing up to my level, the second floor. It only had four apartments on this and the third floor and my lovely neighbor's door was the second door that *he* knocked on. Hers was also the first door to open. My heart sank.

With her young son in her arms, Sharon opened the door but kept the chain lock on. I could tell by her reaction that she recognized *him* from the description I had given her of *him* just a day and a half earlier. She was amazing! She pretended to not even know me and listened compassionately to *his* version of the story and all about the "crazy lady who took *his* two daughters away from *him*," and how *he* heard that I had moved to this end of the city. She even took *his* information when *he* pleaded with her to please call *him* if she met me anywhere near there. She nodded good-bye and politely closed her door when *he* tried to shake her hand. Then I saw *his* face! It really was *him*! Oh my God! I ran away from the door, knowing that *he* would look for feet behind the door through the gap between the door and the floor if *he* came to our door.

Knock, knock, knock … Knock, knock, knock. That was the other neighbor's door … no answer. My heart felt as if it rose up into my throat, as our door was the next one to receive *his* series of knocks on it. The children stopped playing for a moment when they also heard the knocking. I snuck quietly into their room and sang to them until the knocking, the walking up to the next level, more knocking, and finally *his* snaky shuffle down the stairs and out the rear entrance door led me to believe that *he* had finally left our building. I sat on the floor for a while with the children in their bedroom, and I stretched my neck up enough to peek over the window ledge, not enough for anyone outside to see me though. I saw Phidelopé puff on *his* cigarette and slowly gaze over the entire property before slumping into the driver's seat of *his* car. *He* waited there for another twenty minutes or more before loose gravel spit out from under the tires of *his* car as *he* angrily sped away.

Minutes after that, a delicate knock came to my door. I looked through the door's peephole again with fear that *he* may have come around the front way and was trying to trick me. What relief I felt, and I quickly opened my door to welcome Sharon and her son into our shattered world. She hugged me close and asked me if I wanted to use her phone to call the police.

She kept repeating, "Ridiculous! This is so ridiculous! It's a good thing you told me about *him* and that you shared with me all that you have been through with *him*, because *he* certainly could have convinced anyone else to take pity on *him*. She promised to write the details of *his* encounter with her out on paper for me so I could take it to my next appointment with Désirée and the CAS counselor. She assured me that she would take Victoria and her son to her mother's on that day so *he* wouldn't surprise her again if *he* should reappear while I was out.

I did call the police from her place later that afternoon while she stayed at my place with the children. They said they really couldn't do anything for me until *he* actually harmed me or the children.

"Ridiculous!" is what *I* said that time. It was such a shame that the previous years of abuse that we endured, and finally escaped from, meant nothing now. Any reports to authorities would continue to be my word against *his* until there was actual proof. What was even more *ridiculous* was how CAS planned to get that proof.

I now forgive myself for:

- Not insisting to the police that *he* really was a threat to us
- Not stressing to the police and CAS how cunning, deceitful, and *dangerous* Phidelopé really was.

PEARL OF WISDOM

My calm politeness and respect for people of authority actually worked against me during this fight for our lives! I encourage *you* to speak *up* and *out* for yourself as often and as clearly as you can. Tell *everyone* you can without holding back any details! *Your* life and the life of your child(ren) matters, and *your story needs to be heard*! *Make it count!* You'll be glad you did. I was the tree in the forest that fell, and nobody heard it or cared about it and its broken branches because I didn't tell! *You are the lioness*; get out of the cage and *roar* for your safety and freedom.

CHAPTER 16

Christmas 1984

The weeks that followed this event proved to be quite challenging. My lawyer was insisting that I clarify issues of child support and possibly spousal support, and the CAS counselor had to reschedule two prearranged appointments with Désirée and me.

I managed to find some joy when I did meet the other neighbors on our floor, and they all loved the costumes that Désirée and Victoria were dressed up in for their first Halloween. This gave me hope that our lives could be normal just as soon as the legal separation was finalized and we could dismiss the craziness with CAS. We were assigned a new counselor, a young, inexperienced female who briefly familiarized herself with our case. She set up our next meeting, the one in which Desirée would "play" with the sexually correct dolls, for the following week.

I explained to her how discouraging the inconsistency of CAS personnel and our appointments was to me. I expressed how hard I had worked to leave all of this behind us in order to forget about the tragic past and to move forward with our lives—*without* being reminded about our past. Working with CAS was a constant reminder of our past. She was not empathetic, and she insisted that we come to the next appointment an extra fifteen minutes early to properly prepare the rooms. I politely agreed to this, and then Désirée and I took another long bus ride back to our apartment. Thankfully, Sharon always greeted us with a welcoming smile, a friendly hug, and a warm cup of tea for me to sip as she listened to my struggles, while our children played together in the safety and comfort of her apartment.

I was grateful to have enough money from the welfare benefits that finally kicked in to pay our rent, which included heat and water. I was able to feed my family healthy food, and if we had any money left over at the end of the month, I would take them for a stroll to have lunch at a family restaurant just a little down the street. This was our treat. As we were preparing to leave for this treat one afternoon, I was surprised to meet *his* father in the hallway.

I liked Phidelopé's family, and I had encouraged them to stay in touch with me so they would not have to lose touch with their first grandchildren. It wasn't their fault, after all. I wished, at that moment, that *his* father would have given me some advance notice. However, I still didn't have a phone, so it was easy to forgive this surprise visit. I welcomed him in, but he nervously refused and insisted that he and his wife just wanted to take Désirée for the day. Their plan was to take her to visit Désirée's great-grandparents in Kipming, and they would bring her back to me later on that evening. The hair on the back of my head stood up in disbelief of what I was hearing.

I didn't like the sound of this at all and I asked him, "Is Phidelopé in the vehicle that you and your wife are traveling in?"

"Oh, no, no, no … It's just the two of us," he replied nervously.

"Great then," I said. "Have her come up, and we'll all visit here in our apartment. I'm sure the children will be happy to spend time with both of you."

"Okay," he said with a smile from ear to ear. He rushed down the stairs and out the door and sat in the car to discuss this with his wife. His head hung low when he returned, saddened by her insistence to *not* enter our apartment.

"Well," I said optimistically, "we'll bring the kids, along with me, to her in your car, and we'll have a little visit there! Okay?"

She was clearly unhappy with our solution; however, the rest of us made the best of a challenging situation.

They hugged their granddaughters tightly and wiped away tears as we said our good-byes. I had no idea that this would be their last visit with us in Hapland.

I received one support payment on November 1 of $126 in the form of a certified check through registered mail. I was not impressed. My lawyer explained the breakdown like this: "The $125 is *his* monthly child support, and child support does *not* grant *him* access to *his* children. We're still working with CAS for that. The other $1 is alimony and is something the courts set in motion in case *he* miraculously gets a job or comes into money; then you would be allowed a portion of that increase but only for the next two years because you were only married for two years."

I chuckled in dismay, and I maintained that I did not want *his* drug-dealing money. She insisted that I accept it, and she wanted me to fight for more. Ironically, the December personal check from *him* bounced, and I didn't even bother to tell her that. I was exhausted with fighting, and I begged her to just move forward with legalizing the separation so I could then apply for a divorce. She hung her head, not willing to accept my surrender, and then she dumped the next plan on me.

"Well," she said, "as you know, Désirée was the first child in our district to work with CAS and sexually correct dolls. *His* lawyer viewed the recorded session and deemed it to be inconclusive."

I burst into tears as I vividly remembered questioning the whole process with the sexually correct dolls, my daughter, and the CAS caseworker at the time. I found it odd that only she and Désirée entered a room, while I stood behind a mirrored wall in an adjoining room. I had to watch my toddler show that caseworker things that I never imagined any little girl would think was normal interaction between a child and her father. I was mortified, and I cried helplessly watching from that cold room, watching in disbelief as she clearly identified herself as the little girl doll and *him*, the adult male doll, as Daddy. She undressed both dolls and told the CAS caseworker that that was how they would sleep together. It was freaky to see how she placed the Daddy doll's penis into the little girl doll's vagina and how she said it hurts her, but Daddy says, "Only at first ... not for long."

I looked around in disbelief and asked the person in the room with me, "How much more of this do you need for your *proof*?" I was furious!

She said she would inquire, and then she left the room. I watched the interaction with her and the CAS caseworker in the mirrored room next door, and I was relieved when they wound down the playtime with the sexually correct dolls and slowly returned my twenty-seven-month-old daughter to me. I prayed that we would *never* have to return there. I praised Désirée for her good playtime with that lady, and I promised to take her and her sister for ice cream as soon as we got home. And I did!

These vivid memories were interrupted with my lawyer's impatient voice. "So we have to send them both for a proof visit." Without hesitation, she continued, "It will be set up over Christmas at *his* parent's place. They will supervise the whole visit, and the children will have their own beds—a crib for Victoria. Okay?"

"No!" I cried, "This is *not* okay!" In disbelief, I asked for clarity. "So you, the courts, and CAS want me to agree to let my helpless children go back to *him,* in a city three hours away from me, with *his* family who hasn't seen them for almost two months, to be with *him*? No. I refuse to allow this! I have seen what *he* did to her at twenty-two months young! And from what the video showed, that was probably not the only time! This proof visit is not right! My children will have to suffer because a lawyer feels the evidence in unclear? Seriously?! This cannot be the solution! And you want me to agree with that?"

"Yes." She stated firmly. "You have no choice if you want to refuse shared custody."

"Of course I want to refuse shared custody! It's clear that *he's* a danger to children!"

"Yes," she finally agreed. "But I'm afraid this has to happen. Please have the children ready for *him* and his sister to pick them up on December 23rd. They will return the children to you on December 26th at noon. Immediately upon their return to you, you must take them to the emergency department at the hospital for examination for sexual abuse. When the receptionist asks you why you are bringing them in, you are to simply state, 'incest,' and they'll know what to do. Do you understand?"

I nodded and mumbled with my head to my chest, "Yes."

I prayed that something horrible would happen to *him* and that none of this would have to happen. But another one of my mother's sayings rang through with truth again: "Bad things seem to only happen to good people." We were all about to experience that because the courts forced us to!

That was and still is the worst Christmas of my life and little Désirée's and Victoria's too.

Friends of mine who owned a car were visiting with me when *he* and *his* sister returned my children to me that December 26th, 1984. No one spoke as they, *he* and *his* sister, deposited the children into our new living room, now across the street from where we had first settled. I held Désirée in my arms and watched as *his* sister placed Victoria, still strapped in her car seat, onto the floor in the living room. She gave me a dirty look upon exiting, and *he* smugly smiled at me as *he* waved good-bye to *his* children.

Without hesitation, we gathered the children up and made our way to the hospital as soon as we saw them speed off in a cloud of freshly disturbed snow.

There was a highly unusual commotion as the nurse whisked me and my two children off to a separate room and seriously questioned my statement of incest upon our arrival. She nervously reminded me that CAS would be contacted, and the doctor would have to examine the children. I boldly reminded her that, "Yes, I was quite aware that CAS would be contacted and that my children would be examined for sexual abuse! They, CAS, are the reason my children had to go through all of this! *Yes!* Please, once and for all, *get your proof!* Please don't mess anything up because we can *never* do this again!"

The time it took to all unfold was a blur. Our stress was met with deep sadness and ironic relief as the doctor confirmed sexual penetration on twenty-nine-month-old Désirée, and some sort of fondling was possible with seven-month-old Victoria. There it was … *proof!* I don't remember what time it was when we got home. I only remember making a silent promise to myself, and my children, that we would never see that family again. I also promised to do everything in my power to make our lives forever better—forever better!

I still cry with this memory.

Legally separated, divorced, marriage annulled, done!

I now forgive myself for:

- All the wrongs that had to happen to get life right
- Being helpless in so many unforgivable situations
- Half-believing that *he* wouldn't dare to mistreat our children right under *his* families' noses
- Not challenging the court's decisions

PEARL OF WISDOM

There's a saying, "You'll get through it if you're brought to it." This, ironically, is true. Please know that you are not alone! You, with the support of a trusted professional, a true friend, your *God*, faith in your prayers, and revived faith in *yourself*, will get through it. It's a journey. Pack your courage, persistence, daring determination, tears and fears, intuition, self-love, and newfound wisdom, because it's a path that's filled with distractions, guilt, ups, and downs. Just when you think you've got it licked, another layer of emotion will surface for you to meet with courage, and you will learn to find peace again. You will love again. You will trust again. You must; otherwise, *your abuser wins. When you don't move forward and upward, you merely exist to physically die the emotional death that you already experienced!*

CHAPTER 17

Along Came a Clown

Creating a normal life for me and my little girls was my only focus. I secretly hated men; even aspects of my father and my brother annoyed me. This was actually a survival phase for me that kept us safe during the next few years. I was super vigilant, and I only allowed strong, wise women and their children into our world. I treasure the friendships and support from Nell and Cassandra from the second floor, Marie-Lynne and Cora from across the hall, and Kara and Melanie next door to me. Over time, I grew to trust Brian in the bachelor's apartment down the hallway directly in front of our apartment just past the laundry room and Kara's kind and gentle husband, Matt.

Thank goodness I did, because a few months of peace and quiet and not hearing from *him* nor anyone and *his* family was suddenly interrupted when I saw *him* in his car slink past our main-floor living room window. I immediately gathered up Désirée and Victoria and desperately knocked on Kara's apartment door. We barreled into her apartment as soon as the door opened, and I rushed down the hallway to the first bedroom on the left and hushed the children. She followed in silence as I held my finger over my lips to signal her silence too. Once we settled down, I whispered to her the threat that was now lurking in our hallways. Her eyes opened wide; she knew our story well. She immediately called Brian down the hall from my apartment, and together, they shared what they could see through the peepholes in their doors. They watched *him* as *he* first knocked on our apartment door. *He* stood there, impatiently tapping one foot. When there was no response, *he* knocked on Brian's door. Brian held his breath and did not answer.

The silent pause on the phone alarmed Kara, so she whispered, "Are you okay, Brian?"

After a long moment, he responded, "Yes. *He's* still in the building! *He's* in the laundry room having a cigarette."

They stayed on the line together as Brian kept watch through the peephole in his door. A few moments later, he whispered, "Okay, he's leaving the laundry room and checking Itzabella's door ... Oh my God! ... *He's* inside her apartment! *He* left the door open, and I can see *him* checking out all the rooms! Do you want me to call the police?"

Kara whispered these details to me, and I said, "Yes! Please!"

A loud knock came to Kara's door before she could relay the urgent response to Brian, so he listened intently as Kara kept the phone line open while she talked to Phidelopé through the space of her chain-locked door. Once again, *he* shared *his* sad, soapy story, this time to a new neighbor.

She politely nodded as she patiently listened and then dismissed this stranger with a polite response to *his* search for us: "We're all really private in this building. No one speaks to each other. I really don't know exactly whom you are inquiring about. Perhaps you should go to the police with your situation." With that, she gently closed the door and began to play with her daughter, as if nothing unusual was affecting their lives. What a blessing!

I almost burst out laughing when she suggested that he take his concern to the police.

Brian piped up again, "*He's* still lurking. Keep Itzabella and the girls there. I'm gonna go out for a smoke and invite *him* to join me outside. I'll stay with *him* until *he* leaves. Okay?"

"Sure," Kara replied. "Take *him* out front so we can watch from here. I'll notify the police if *he* tries to come back in."

They hung up their phones, and we watched for a long time. One cigarette turned into two as Phidelopé babbled on. Brian only listened. They shook hands, and *he* finally got back into *his* car and sped away. Brian joined us in Kara's apartment, and we played with the children for hours to pretend that all was well. Brian returned to his apartment when Matt came home, and we stayed for supper at Kara and Matt's place that evening. It's a good thing we did because *he* returned. This time, mighty Matt, greeted *him* at the front entrance with a stern, "Hey Mister, you are not welcome here!"

With a cordless receiver in his hand, Matt indicated his clear intention to call the police if *he* stepped past him.

Thankfully, Phidelopé retreated to *his* car, and we *never* saw *him* again.

Through mirror work, exercise, meditation, and happy visits with friends and family, my self-confidence returned. My children also blossomed in our positive environment. Our circle of friends grew as we celebrated birthdays, ventured out to local beaches during the summer, and shared joy, laughter, and warm hot chocolate with bright, beautiful souls through the winter months. On my twenty-fourth birthday, my friends arranged for sweet Cassandra, who was now a young teenager, to babysit Désirée and Victoria while a group of my friends took me out to a new hot spot to dance and celebrate my young adult life. That's where I met the clown.

Nestor was a lively, high-spirited, witty guy who danced his way to our table. He knew some of my friends, and they welcomed him and his two other friends to join us. He made everyone laugh and would enthusiastically spin my girlfriends around on the dance floor whenever a good tune would shake up the crowd. Eventually, it was my turn to dance with him. I was ashamed of my lack of rhythm and two left feet, but it didn't bother him at all. He smiled and sang the words to the song, cheerfully mimicking the emotions that the happy song was intended to create.

I was happy to see that his good mood was not alcohol related; he was sweating more from dancing compared to the amount of alcohol that he only sipped from time to time. He took up conversation with my friend Kylie sitting next to me, so she politely introduced him to me. I shook his hand and gleefully shared my name and that I was a single mother of two beautiful children. Secretly, this was my weapon, intended to scare off any man who would not take interest in a woman in my situation. It didn't bother him at all. He told me how he had numerous nieces and nephews and how much he treasured being their favorite uncle. I was cautiously impressed.

Nestor, the clown, entertained us all until closing time. My friend Kylie, who was going to stay at my place that night and happily maintained her self-appointed sober diver status, enthusiastically invited Nestor and his buddies over to my place for coffee. They politely accepted and remained calm to not wake up my sleeping children during their brief visit and quick cup of coffee.

The door was just locked shut when Kylie blurted out, "I think he likes you!"

Confused and surprised at the thought of anyone even being interested in me, I asked, "Who?'"

"Nestor!" she exclaimed.

I laughed at her and declared that I didn't think I would ever welcome another man into our lives. Ironically, while we were out, a dozen red roses in a beautiful vase were delivered to my apartment with a card attached to it that said, "Happy Birthday! ... From your secret admirer." The gesture clearly indicated that other men were interested in me. Kylie laughed at the irony of it all. She was single with no children and more than ready for a relationship, while I, a single mom with two children ... getting attention from men, was *not* open to the idea of a relationship at all.

The idea of a relationship softened the next day when Nestor knocked at the door. It was the afternoon, and Kylie opened the door to him while I was feeding the girls a healthy snack. His loud laughter filled the room as he and Kylie cheerfully greeted each other. Then, in a heartbeat, he whisked right past me with a quick, "Hello."

He then picked up a Kermit the Frog toy and, in Kermit's character voice, began to play with the girls. They were delighted with his childlike joy and accepted his friendship without hesitation. He kept them entertained for a half hour and then politely dismissed himself. He thanked me for letting him play with them and commented on how lucky I was to have such beautiful, intelligent little girls. Bewildered at all that had just taken place, I thanked him too.

He glanced quickly at the roses on the table and shyly asked if I was in a relationship.

I looked over at the roses from my mystery man and said, "No, not at the moment."

He smiled and walked away, whistling as he exited the building.

A five-year relationship blossomed from that encounter, and on Saturday, August 24, 1991, we got married.

I am now grateful for:

- The precious time I took to heal
- The amazing friends who supported me and my children on our journey to serenity and happiness

PEARL OF WISDOM

"Seek and you shall find." When you find peace in your world through forgiveness, sincere support, faith, and self-love, you open up to receive the blessings that you prayed for.

CHAPTER 18

Ball and Chain

During the years prior to our wedding, Nestor was a fun-loving, kind, considerate, compassionate gentleman toward me. To Désirée and Victoria, he was a human jungle gym, swinging them up, down, and all around him in a frenzy of laughter and excitement. He worked long hours during the weekdays and would make time for us on weekends.

I made it clear to Nestor that we would not live together during our courtship. I figured if he could support himself and maintain a healthy relationship with us while we got to know and trust each other, then he would be able to support a family if and when we decided to get married. A true test of his commitment to us occurred when I enrolled in a one-year, full-time Certified Medical Nurse Course at Acadine College. That was a busy year for us. I, along with Désirée and Victoria, had moved to a public housing two-bedroom apartment, and Désirée was going into a full-day senior kindergarten class, while Victoria was enrolled for half days in junior kindergarten and half days at day care. My schedule was full days at the college and one evening a week in the medical lab. It was a good test.

I found his request to use the grant money I had received as a mature student to purchase a brand-new car rather odd. It would be in his name, but I could use it instead of taking the city bus. Even with his promise to repay me, my intuition sensed some doubt. He certainly had a way of getting what he wanted when he really wanted something. This was a red flag that I was too busy to address at the time.

I met his pleas for my attention with adult reasoning. If he shared in half of the responsibilities that my busy schedule now demanded of me, such as helping with the dishes and laundry while I did homework with Désirée and bathing the two children before putting them to bed at night, then I could spare an hour with him before beginning my nightly homework assignments. It wasn't long before we saw less of Nestor. I really didn't mind; I was dedicated to the children's welfare and maintaining excellence in my course and career choice. I chose medical assisting because it fulfilled my longing for a career of caring for people. It also met my need to find such a field in which I could be employed on a full-time basis that would also allow me to have evenings and weekends open for my children. I was thrilled to have passed the entrance exams, and nothing would deter me from this empowering leap forward, not even Nestor's increasing gambling debts and his uncalled-for jealousy.

An unwelcome surprise of the college going on strike during my second month into the course almost deflated my bubble of ambitious dreams. Acting on a wise tip from an enthusiastic nursing student to call the physician who was sponsoring her in the registered nurse program proved to be a positive move for me—one that secured my future employment at that office upon graduation from the medical assisting program.

Nestor's insane jealousy of the one male, married, mature student in our class and the physician who hired me during the college strike and guaranteed me a job upon graduation, coupled with his increasing deception about his financial challenges, led me to end our relationship and call off our engagement.

This decision was met with much disapproval from my parents and my sister. They felt that I was insane to end a relationship with a man who didn't mind getting involved with a woman who had two children from an unhealthy past, and they scolded me with their words. My sister even wrote me a lengthy letter expressing her opinion that I was making a big mistake and that I was becoming overconfident. My father's final insult was him telling me, "No one will ever buy the cow if he's getting the milk for free!" That proved to be the breaking point for me. I couldn't believe that my father had such an opinion of me! None of my family members knew about the numerous arguments that Nestor and I had over money and his insane, unwarranted jealousy. When he showed up at my door one evening after I had put the children to bed and my energy was deplete from studying for exams, I agreed to resume our relationship. He was on his best behavior, and we agreed to marry once I graduated.

The week off from the job that I had just begun in June 1991 allowed for our brief honeymoon that August. During our honeymoon, his gambling, deception, and jealousy resurfaced.

Upon on our exit from the church on our wedding day, he declared, "Well, I guess I now have a ball and chain!" Those words were now haunting me.

The ring was fresh on my finger, and he immediately became insecure about being committed to one woman for the rest of his life. Nestor danced with all the beautiful women at our wedding reception to everyone's delight but mine. People even questioned me if I was jealous of this.

"Me, jealous? No, that's his thing! He's just a big flirt in a red shirt," was my honest reply. I had no idea at that time that this was going to be a problem.

We worked well to provide a loving family life for our children, and we bought a home within our first year of marriage. Life was good, and I felt pressured to provide him with a child of his own. I was able to walk to work, and my job began much earlier than his. This meant that he had to step up his responsibilities by getting Désirée and Victoria up and ready for school before he went to work. This was met with much resistance from him, and our efforts in procreation were negatively affected. Two spontaneous miscarriages were another red flag that I ignored. This, coupled with his loud and obnoxious remarks that expressed his immature disapproval of my employer, led me to apply for a job in public health. My level of maturity and ability to effectively communicate in both French and English granted me the position as Medical Health Educator in Public Health. A significant pay increase, health benefits, and summers off lifted a lot of tension in our marriage. A successful pregnancy seemed to be our reward.

Christmas 1993 was one of heightened emotions as I went into premature labor during midnight mass. I was admitted to hospital to stop the contractions and avoid a premature delivery of our baby who was only due to arrive in March 1994. Désirée and Victoria sat and sadly observed our friends' children open their Christmas presents following midnight mass. This was their tradition, and we were just relieved that they agreed to take our girls overnight. We were very uncertain of what was next for the first few hours following my admittance to hospital.

Nestor left the hospital once I was stable. Thankfully, I was dismissed from the hospital the next morning. We picked up our sad children from our friends' place, and we were all pleasantly surprised when we entered our home that Christmas morning.

"Santa did visit our place during the night, after all!" the children joyously exclaimed.

I was equally surprised with the number of presents that appeared under our Christmas tree because, just the week prior to all of this, Nestor had expressed his lack of success when he gambled away all of the Christmas money. I had saved that money for months. I gave it to him *specifically* to shop for presents for the children.

This was the beginning of another sad and super-challenging time in our lives. Many nights, even following the birth of Janelle on Sunday, March 6, 1994 at 5:18 p.m., I would fall asleep upset with myself for making similar bad decisions ten years following the positive changes that I worked tirelessly and consciously for. I fooled myself by settling, by accepting less for myself because I wanted my sister to love me and my parents to approve of me. I settled because at least he wasn't physically and sexually abusive to me or my daughters. I did not know then how damaging his mental and emotional abuse of me would prove to be.

Soon, I represented more than just his ball and chain to him. I became his excuse for coming home even later at night, for his struggle to quit smoking, for his habit of gambling, and for his decision to join a dart league each winter and play golf each summer. I begged him to be more present in our lives, and I was pleased when he agreed to coach a local girls' baseball team of which Désirée and Victoria were team players. This joy was squashed at the end of the season when Victoria came home upset from the championship banquet, and through tears and frustration, she expressed her disgust with her dad (Nestor) because he had flirted and danced all night with her friend's newly separated mom. The air of distrust lingered even when we moved to a new, bigger home in the city, away from that family.

The children frequently expressed their feelings of not belonging there with. "Mom, it feels like the real owners will come home any day now."

Over time, I became seriously ill and lost my job in public health. I was grateful to be welcomed to return to the medical practice in Landercal; ironically, everyone there now met Nestor's approval. My health continued to deteriorate, and I began to have fainting spells at work. My physician referred me to a neurologist in Toronto, and on January 29, 2001, Nestor and I drove through an incredibly frightening snowstorm to be on time for my consultation at St. Maria's Hospital the next morning. The relief I felt when we finally settled into our hotel room that night was short-lived.

"You like it like this. That's how *he* did it to you. Right?" This was the arrogant remark that Nestor made upon hiking my flannelette granny gown over my head and raping me.

I kept saying, "No! No! No!"

I even bargained with him to wait until the morning, but no way … He insisted and persisted. I became numb. I left my body emotionally, mentally, and spiritually, and I resolved to *never* let him touch me again after that.

The purpose for the lumbar puncture and testing that I experienced the next day didn't matter anymore. Upon our return home, I moved Victoria's bed into the bedroom that she would now share with Désirée, and I created a new safe haven for myself.

I applied the skills that I was learning through Reiki to heal my whole self. My self-confidence and empowerment grew each day. What a blessing this proved to be, especially the evening that I received a disturbing phone call.

She was a blast from the past. The pitch of her voice told me that she was desperate for answers. She begged to find resolve through a visit with me, Désirée, and Victoria. It was Phidelopé's little sister,

Nancy, on the phone. She was leaving her husband whom she'd found making out with their babysitter, and she was traveling with their two children to get away from him. They were passing through Hapland, and she felt that a visit with us would help her find answers to her murky past. She hoped that this clarity would set her upon her own healing path. I discussed this with Désirée and Victoria, which also led me to tell them the truth about our journey to freedom.

Through tears, mommy hugs, and breathing into calmness the truth was finally revealed to them. It lifted a heavy burden from my heart, head, and body; it was a freeing experience.

Désirée was also relieved, as it helped her to understand the disturbing dreams and odd feelings that she had been experiencing all her life. She never knew how to discuss them with me or anyone else.

Victoria was mostly angry, and her feisty-spirited solution was expressed when she said, "Mom, is Désirée going to be okay? Are her insides okay? You're sure he just touched me, right? Oh man! He's gotta pay for this! Did he go to jail? Is he on the list? He owes us, Mom!"

I calmed her with reassurance that all that needed to be done had been done, and we were wise to let that sleeping giant continue to sleep. "We are safe now and away from all of that," I reassured them. "So, do you two want to speak to Nancy, or shall we just wish her well?" I asked Désirée and Victoria as I considered the next obstacle to tackle.

Their answer was compassionate. "Mom, please have her come over. You need to tell her *everything*!"

What an amazingly emotional reunion we all had. Nestor took Nancy's son and daughter to play downstairs with him and Janelle, while Désirée, Victoria, and I huddled together on the big living room sofa with Nancy. Courageously, I told her the *truth* of our entire experience with Phidelopé. I hugged her and asked for her forgiveness as she expressed how she felt that she was responsible for our broken marriage. She thought she did something wrong on our bus ride together to Kipming all those years ago. Through tears of relief, I asked her how this would help her. In a light bulb moment, she expressed, "That's why I could not remember anything before age eleven. I now remember that our Pépère did things, sexual things, to me! I wonder if he did this to all of us … to Phidelopé too?"

She blew her nose and looked up at us. We were all stunned with this revelation. We had a group hug for a long time and cried healing tears for as long as we needed to.

Nancy then looked into her nieces' eyes and said, "That's not an excuse for what *he* has done! I am so sorry *he* hurt you."

She then turned to me, looked into my eyes, and with a big sigh of relief, she said, "Thank you for your bravery. You did nothing wrong. I now know what I have to do."

We hugged one more long time, and then she gathered up her beautiful little children, and they continued on their journey. We all wished her well, and then they were gone.

Désirée's nineteenth birthday wish set a new goal in motion for me. She expressed her frustration and wisdom with this statement: "Mom, I want the same gift that I asked for last year, and I am so disappointed that I still haven't received it."

Confused and saddened, I responded. "I don't understand—what did we miss?"

She reminded me. "I asked you to leave Dad (Nestor) last year, Mom. We have been watching you die a slow and painful death. If you believe you have to stay married for the sake of us kids, you're wrong. We would rather have you stay alive by living apart from each other than to struggle to stay together for the sake of marriage, family, and what others would think of you. I love you, Mom, and leaving this miserable lie of a life would save us all. Will I get my birthday wish this year?"

Through tears of immense relief, I congratulated my wise Earth Angel daughter, hugged her, and whispered in her ear, "Yes, my dear; you'll get your wish. I'll talk to Nestor tonight and tell your sisters in the morning."

God, the angels, and Mother Nature certainly supported me and Nestor through our difficult discussion with our three little Earth Angels the morning of August 12, 2001. I was relieved that Nestor was in agreement to legally separate, and he let me take the lead to break this news to Désirée, Victoria, and Janelle as they sat, huddled together on our comfy sofa in our living room. The room grew dark as purple-gray clouds filled the skies. The wind picked up, and during the heart-wrenching news flash to the girls, we watched our patio furniture bounce furiously down our neighborhood street. By the completion of delivering the difficult news, the wind, hail, and thunder had cleared, and much like the relief expressed by embracing our truth and embarking upon a new, lighter chapter of our lives, sunshine lit up our living room, and a bright, cheerful rainbow arched through the clear blue sky. Clearly, this decision was celebrated, and our new direction was the pot of gold at the end of the rainbow that poured into our living room.

By November of that year, I had moved into a three-bedroom apartment, and I only took what I would need to begin anew. Nestor stayed in the house that never felt like home to me and the girls, because he needed more time to adapt to the change. We shared custody and visitation with the girls. Désirée chose to go live with a friend in her sincere intention to not offend either parent, while Victoria and Janelle adapted to our new residence and were happy to return to their familiar rooms whenever they visited Nestor.

The chain was broken, and this ball was free to roll on … and I did!

I now forgive myself for:

- Cowering to pressure from my sister and my father
- Marrying another man whom I really didn't love
- Having his baby to reward him for marrying me
- Setting myself back to square one
- Allowing my own feelings of what I thought I did wrong to keep me silent for so long

PEARL OF WISDOM

Just because you may feel shame for your mistakes, it doesn't mean that you cannot recognize faults or mistakes in others. Address issues sooner than I did. You'll be glad you did.

Forgiveness also means forgiving yourself!

CHAPTER 19

Evolving

Time really does heal all wounds. For this, I am very grateful!

As I embraced my empowerment through Reiki and counseling, I began to evolve. I found the courage to leave the amazing team of medical professionals, who truly became my other family, in order to build my own Reiki practice. I am still amazed by how it all unfolded.

During a pleasant morning at the medical center, I was expressing to my best friend and co-worker how crazy anyone would be to leave this amazing, forward-moving medical practice where every team member truly loved their roles and supported each other to professionally provide the best care to the friendliest and most loyal patients, and then—*poof*—within a month, I was magically propelled to hand in my letter of resignation. It is amazing how powerfully and miraculously the universe and divine guidance supported me once I committed to the service of others through teaching Reiki and treating clients on a full-time basis.

I took this leap of faith on October 1, 2004. I remember waking up that first morning and declaring myself as Itzabella Katchastarr, Reiki Master. I was thrilled and appreciative of the skills, work ethic, exceptional personal growth, and leadership that I had experienced through professional development events over the past fifteen years through the medical profession, and especially the serenity and empowerment that I developed through my Reiki training. Now, I was ready to fully embrace and live my passionate purpose.

Word of mouth brought numerous clients to me, and I evolved even more. Being a messenger of truth, I embarked upon the journey to legally change my name.

I was baptized with the name Itzabella, and I grew up happily knowing who I was with that name. My first legal name change came with the unhappiest marriage to the rapist. Thankfully, that marriage was annulled. I kept Phidelopé's family name until I married Nestor. Then, with that marriage, my name changed again. An unpleasant divorce from Nestor granted me permission to change my name once more. Most people usually revert back to their maiden name. That was not the path for me. I prayed that my parents and family members would not be insulted when I chose to legally change my name to Itzabella Katchastarr.

The name Katchastarr truly represented my evolution. I actually wanted to legally change my name to only be "Starr," not Itzabella Katchastarr. Starr is truly all that really felt sincere to me. I approached my children about this idea, and they supported my choice of Itzabella Katchastarr; however, they strongly disagreed with my desire for Starr to be my only name. They said, "Mom, you are already weird enough! You can't just be known as Starr ... You're not like Cher or Madonna. Please don't embarrass us."

Reluctantly, I honored their sensitivity to the issue and began the legal process to identify myself as Itzabella Katchastarr and eliminate the name that I acquired through my abusive marriage to Nestor. I felt immediate relief upon mailing the documents.

"Yay!" I said to myself. "Now I can truly step into the person I have evolved to be."

A speed bump along this journey of transformation occurred when I received a letter from our government explaining that I needed the permission of my ex-husband to grant this name change. I was deeply insulted and not ready for the challenges that this new development presented. It pleased Nestor to hold the key to challenge my endeavor to embrace this change, to be myself—my true self.

He avoided every opportunity to see me in person, even when he came to pick up our daughter for visitation. He would make arrangements with the neighbor to have her at their place for the pickup time. This went on for months. When I explained to my neighbor what was happening, she found a way to convince him to follow her to my place to get an item for our daughter, and when he stepped into my place, I presented him with the permission document. Initially he met me and this trap, as he called it, with loud resistance. Miraculously, through my neighbor's calming words of wisdom, he surrendered and signed the document.

I still breathe a sigh of relief as I remember how uplifting I felt as I mailed this life-enhancing document. Carrying anyone else's name felt like ownership to me, and going *back* to my own maiden name made me feel as a though I was stepping backward into my childhood identity, and that no longer fit for me.

One friend laughed when I told her what I was doing, and she commented, "If anything, you should change your name to Chaos!"

She went on to explain that pure chaos was how my life looked to her. I paused for a moment and then thanked her for her honesty. I agreed with her opinion that to the outside world, my life, up to that point, would truly look and feel chaotic to others. Then

I shared with her how I chose the name Katchastarr. It unfolded like this:

When I was around six years old, I was downstairs sitting with my mother as we watched my father build a beautiful log wall to divide the recreation room from the laundry area. My mother began to sing a favorite song of mine. "Catch a shiny star and put it in your pocket, save it for a rainy day ..."

I began to enthusiastically sing along with her. At one point, she changed the usual sound of the song with a higher pitch. This confused me, so I stopped singing along. She encouraged me to continue the way I was singing the song and explained that she was harmonizing. I loved the new sound of the song, and we joyfully sang it over and over again ... in harmony. I always smile when I remember how joyful harmonizing felt for me. Right from that moment, the "Catch a Shiny Star" song was profound for me!

As my life unfolded, as miserable and chaotic as it was at times, I found peace and calmness as I prayed. I prayed and prayed and prayed! I, often with tears streaming down my face, would call upon God, Jesus, Mother Mary, archangels, and angels to guide me to safety, to peaceful solutions for my rainy days, and blessings for all those I loved. This brought calmness to the drama and chaos, and I clearly would hear, in that knowing place within me ... in my very heart and soul, the divine guidance that I prayed for. Through the years, I took great comfort in knowing that even as a single mom often feeling alone, especially on gloomy, rainy days, I was never alone. The memory of my mother singing that song and the uplifting voices of divine guidance were always there. This brought me to embrace Katchastarr as my name, because with each challenge that I face, I catch a shiny star and put it in my pocket, and I get through my rainy days. Through all that I have experienced to evolve to this beautiful place in my life, I truly did turn chaos into peace and joy as I embraced heavenly guidance.

I now forgive myself for:

- All the times that I felt guilty for not honoring my parents by not reverting to my maiden name
- Succumbing to pressure to save my children from embarrassment and *not* sticking to my heart's desire to just be named Starr

Gratitude:

I am forever grateful for the divine support and guidance that empowered me to make this change.

I am grateful that after two years of my parents' refusal to speak to me, they finally asked me why I changed my name, and they let go of the insult they carried in their belief that I was not proud to be their daughter. When I explained to them that it was truly because of them and the profound experience of harmonizing that special song with Mom that I chose the name Katchastarr, they came to appreciate me and my choice. Thank God!

PEARL OF WISDOM

I encourage *you* to fully embrace who you are and to listen to the call of your soul for the name that clearly defines whom you have evolved into on your journey to fulfillment. I am already so happy for you! Embrace and enjoy your truth.

CHAPTER 20

A Test

On December 17, 2004, during a whiteout snowstorm, I graciously tipped the moving team who struggled to successfully maneuver the final item—my turn-of-the-century upright piano—into my new home.

This amazing place, Healing House, clearly proved the effectiveness and magnificence of journaling my positive affirmations, mantras, sincere gratitude, and the clarity of thought that I had been focusing upon from the time I had received a rent increase notice. This excerpt from a my personal journal clearly helped me with the process of releasing fear and getting clear on all that I desired to experience in order to enhance my life and my experiences with my children. The desires that I had for the best experience for my clients and my expanding Reiki practice also became clear to me.

JOURNALING

This is what I wrote in my journal when I decided to get clear about all that I desired to experience in my life.

Saturday, June 2, 2003

Wow! Six months to Christmas. Isn't it funny how nobody wants to hear that right now, yet in five months we'll all be caught up in the frenzy and excitement of that special day? Much like my life right now, I know I must create positive change in my life so I can get excited about all that I truly deserve and desire to experience rather than focus on what's missing or what went wrong. The truth is everything is perfectly all right. As I get clear about all that honors me, and my highest good, my life will only get better! Without further hesitation, I now choose to do what it takes to get what I desire and deserve in life: ASK!

"Angels, please help me to create an honest list that truly honors me and helps me to get clear about all that I desire to experience in my life."

"I do things to please myself as well as others, and I am clear about all that I desire to experience in my life." This is the answer the Angels gave me.

I desire to experience ...

- Honesty
- Respect
- True unconditional and passionate love
- Joy in my heart
- Peace in my mind
- Serenity in my soul
- Harmony in mind, body, and spirit
- Excellent health
- Prosperity and wealth
- Security in love, finances, family, friends, employment now and in the future for myself, and my children

At this point, I heard a loud sigh as the Angels began to express their impatience with me and they said, "All this is very true and oh so sweet and sincere, now get clear! As Doreen Virtue has shared in her book *Messages from Your Angels*, "It's not selfish to desire a better life.""

With that influence, I considered the precious lessons in my life and easily focused on what I learned, and I turned the painful experiences into a positive influence. Only I could create change in my life, and so this is more of what I clearly chose.

- I desire to share my life with a man who is loving, caring, considerate, compassionate, patient, and educated in life skills, as well as academically.
- Intellectually we match and are very comfortable with each other.
- He is humbly confident, secure in whom he is and all that he does.
- He is financially responsible and is willing to share his wealth with me and my family.
- He is open, honest, and spiritually connected.
- He loves his family, especially his parents.
- He is at peace with himself and knows where he fits in this world.
- He also contributes back to the people in this world; he is of service to others because he has evolved to this level and loves it!
- He understands knowingness.
- He loves me for exactly who I am. He also loves my children and our dog, and they love him too. He also loves and understands my family, and they love and understand him.
- This man is health conscious, lives well, cares about his appearance, and dresses well. He is handsome

and not conceited. Hygiene is important to him, as is his well-being. He is comfortable with himself. He likes the skin he's in.

- He brings out the best in everyone he knows and meets. He is polite and aware of others' comfort levels.
- He is loyal and trustworthy.
- He is appreciative and expresses this freely and frequently.
- He is generous.
- He loves to love me. He also loves how I love him.
- He is calm, never boring, and definitely not hyper!
- He has a wonderful sense of humor, and his laughter warms my heart.
- He is well-balanced psychologically, emotionally, physically, and spiritually.
- He will take me ballroom dancing.
- He will rub my feet and massage my body.
- He appreciates the gift of Reiki, and he is supportive of my dreams, my accomplishments, and me.
- He is romantic and spontaneous.
- He randomly does acts of kindness.
- He is well organized, neat, and tidy.
- He is easy to live with and a pleasure to be with.
- He spoils me and loves that I spoil him too.
- He is my soul mate, my lover, and my best friend. He is worthy of me, and I am worthy of him, and together we live happily ever after!

"Wow! This feels good." I thought to myself, so I carried on, already feeling much better.

I also desire to:

- Continue working with angels, guides, spirits, etc.
- Work with Doreen Virtue, Louise Hay, and her incredible team of professionals.
- Share insights and pleasant visits with these women and men, and someday the stage.
- Treat Oprah with Reiki and my other special gifts and share with her and her audience the messages that I am guided to share for the highest good of all mankind.
- Swim with dolphins.
- Understand my youngest daughter and someday sing and play guitar together.
- Write books and e-books; create DVDs, CDs, my autobiography, inspirational books, informative books, and children's books.
- Speak publicly, passionately!
- Get paid well to do what I love to do.
- Travel to wonderful places.
- Live wonderful, loving experiences.
- Sleep well, tonight and always!

This may seem rather personal and somewhat lengthy. It is, and that's what yours needs to be too. This way, you become detached from the guilt associated with asking for what you want. You really do feel better as you get clearer and so relieved to finally express, guilt free *all* that you desire and know that you truly deserve.

The really good news is that as soon as you get clear, the universe showers you with all that you desire to experience. Trust and have patience. Let go of expectation. Accept that you are worthy of all good things.

I do have that special man with all of the qualities that I clearly defined in my desire list. I have met and shared special conversations with Doreen Virtue, Louise Hay, and numerous members of Hay House's professional inspirational speakers and authors. I swam with the dolphins on my forty-fourth birthday! I now live happily surrounded by honest, respectful, loving, caring, and supportive individuals. I do understand my youngest daughter; we sing together in the car and laugh out loud often. I have traveled to many wonderful places, and I have plans to travel to many more new and exciting places. I am speaking passionately to numerous people in many public venues with more to come. I am getting paid well while doing all that I love to do. I truly am living wonderful, loving experiences, and I do sleep well. The Oprah thing ... well, I trust that will all happen once she finds out about me!

What a blessing it was to live and pursue my passionate purpose in this dream place that manifested into form *and* to experience real love with the man of my desires.

I remained friends with my former teammates at the medical center, and that was also the place where I entrusted my professional friends to take care of me and my children's health. I maintained my certification as a medical nurse with a promise to be available to that practice if ever the need should arise.

They always welcomed me to celebrate Christmas with them, and for the celebration in 2005, they had a new opportunity for me. I received a call from my dearest friend there. Our conversation began with, "Hi, Itzy. Do you have a date for the Christmas Party?"

"No. I wasn't planning to bring anyone with me. I'm fine by myself," I replied. I quickly followed up. "Please tell me you haven't found someone for me!"

Her giggle told me she had a plan. "Well, actually, we do have someone in mind, and we think you'll be happy about this," she replied.

"Oh no." I retorted. "I am fine on my own, and I'm not sure that I ever want to open up to even think about another relationship!"

She laughed at me. "Life is too short, Itzabella. You don't want to be alone forever, do you?"

At that point in my life, that solution was working. My children were happy and maturing well, and my Reiki practice kept me supported and fulfilled. My experience with relationships helped me to grow; however, the dissatisfaction left a void in my heart that I felt was impossible to ever fill.

My silence led my friend to excitedly pipe up again. "You've met him before! He's so nice, and he's really easy on the eyes."

We laughed simultaneously, and I surrendered. She tweaked my curiosity, so I asked, "Who is he?"

"It's Dr. Yamel!" she expressed enthusiastically. "Remember? Nick? He worked here for a while in 2002."

Surprised, I responded, "Yes. I remember him well. Isn't he married?"

"Not anymore!" she blurted out with laughter and joy.

"Really?!" I was astonished to find this out.

I thanked her for this delightful suggestion and told her that I would think about it and get back to her.

Through the years, Nick and I had also remained friends after I left the medical practice. I even taught him all three levels of Reiki. He and his children came to visit my deaf dog once too. He never revealed anything about his personal life to me; neither one of us did. We respected each other's privacy. He would sometimes email me information that could enhance my practice along with healthy doses of congratulations for my ongoing success.

When we arrived at the Christmas party together, we were welcomed with clapping and enthusiastic remarks that lovingly supported our first date. Our friendship cautiously and patiently evolved into a loving relationship, and I felt so honored when Nick asked me to be present at the lawyer's office, along with him and my former employer and his wife, to legally witness and sign the official purchase documents for the medical practice. He became the new owner, and a new test ensued.

When I embrace a relationship, I do so with all my heart and soul. Thankfully, the past did not interfere with my devotion to this relationship. We both embraced newfound joy in love for each other. We also respected our strengths and individuality as we supported each other's dedication to serve through our blossoming practices.

On June 1, 2010, I received a frantic call from Nick. He humbly asked if I would temporarily handle the duties of office manager at his medical center. He went on to explain that an air of uncertainty was lingering there, and his office manager chose to leave the practice.

"You're the only person who I feel is capable of handling this position," he shared. His faith in my ability, coupled with my admiration and support of him and the team of professionals (my work family) whom I had worked with for fifteen years, led me to say, "Yes. I'll fill the position until you find someone else."

With that, I thanked him for the opportunity. I had to sit down as I became dizzy with thoughts of how I would modify my own practice to serve the needs of his. I calmed myself with reassuring thoughts and conviction that this was just temporary, and I began calling my clients to reschedule them a few weeks into the future. Those few weeks turned into two years, as I put my practice on hold while juggling the growing needs of his medical practice. Nick's wonderful team and the growing number of patients who were attracted to such a pleasant and professional center demanded a lot of my time and energy.

Throughout those two years, I was challenged with serious medical issues:

- Two breast lumpectomies, thankfully benign
- Numerous bladder infections and exploratory procedures
- Right knee surgery
- A complete hysterectomy
- Numerous bouts of laryngitis, as well as ear and respiratory infections
- A life-altering car accident
- Debilitating migraines that led to nonepileptic seizures

I knew that I was not meant to be there doing that job, so I desperately sought a replacement. I began to train a brilliant young nurse who was considering becoming a physician. I shared with her and Nick the importance, and advantage, of learning how to manage a medical practice *before* owning one. They both saw the value in that. I was glad to be supported, and I began to feel some relief. Unfortunately, that relief was met with an emergency on May 24, 2012, when I experienced a stroke.

I now forgive myself for:

- Sacrificing my health, my Reiki practice, and my passionate purpose in order to be of service to my new love's practice
- Accepting a lengthy delay to hire an office manager to replace me
- Ignoring the signs that my deteriorating health was screaming at me to pay attention to myself
- Stepping backward again and *failing the test* to love and honor my self-worth

PEARL OF WISDOM

Please recognize the signs that are happening to you and all around you. Trust your intuition, and love yourself enough to leave any situation that does not honor your highest good. Trust in abundance, and know that you are divinely supported. You will see new opportunities for positive change as soon as you honor your self-worth.

CHAPTER 21

A Stroke of Luck

June 1, 2012, exactly two years from the date when I was hired to temporarily become the medical office manager, I weakly stumbled up the stairs to the home that I shared with Nick. He helped me to settle into the safety and comfort of our home. My doctor had purposely dismissed me from the hospital to avoid possible infection from a life-threatening virus that was sweeping through the hospital at that time. He also emphasized that I was to do *nothing* for the next three months. He left me with follow-up appointments for occupational and physical therapy with specialists in our community who would support me on this journey of recovery.

I only realized the extent of the damage to my brain when I could not count backward by seven and when my memory was challenged with simple exercises that my occupational therapist presented to me. I couldn't even remember the names of my teammates and friends at the medical center.

Following our third appointment, with little progress, the occupational therapist explained that I really needed to give my brain a rest, and she insisted that I not even read any kind of book or magazine article and not revisit writing a book that I had started to write before the car accident. She emphasized the importance of avoiding watching any movies or programs on television that were overstimulating. She also put our sessions on hold for three months. That turned into a bigger challenge than I thought it would be. I learned to appreciate persons who struggle with depression, as I fought that demon too.

Months turned into years. I turned to positive affirmations, visualization techniques, meditation, gentle yoga, and treating myself with Reiki to evolve to a new, wiser, and calmer state of health. Gratitude for my numerous blessings, especially my true friends and loving family members who supported me throughout this transitional time, helped me to realize that this stroke was actually a blessing in disguise. It really was a stroke of luck! It effectively removed me from a job that didn't serve *my highest good*, and it taught me that the world would not fall apart ... even when I did!

I now forgive myself for:

- Striving for perfection faster than my mind and body was able to achieve
- Any embarrassment that I may have brought to friends and family while my memory was so challenged

PEARL OF WISDOM

Please do not allow fear to determine what you do or do not do. Sometimes it feels safer to not embrace change. We convince ourselves that change might disrupt a manageable life. Why make waves? Imagine all the wonderful, peaceful, love, and life that you are missing out on if you don't!

CONCLUSION

— ⚜ —

Rise Above

When I saw *him*, leaning lazily against a wall of the neurologist's clinic on an April morning in 2016—thirty-three years after I'd left Phidelopé, I was instantly and emotionally brought back to those horrific, violent years, and I felt numb. I don't recall how I made it to my neurological appointment. The numerous seizures that ensued for several weeks following this encounter clearly displayed the level of emotional distress I was experiencing. What I had dealt with and healed now violently shook me to the core.

Following the second seizure on that dreadful day, as I lay, exhausted, insulted, and deplete of self-esteem, I called for the nurse who was stationed at the desk near my room at the hospital where I had been admitted for testing.

She quietly drew the curtain closed that separated me from my roommate who was also being tested for a seizure disorder, and she pulled a chair up close to my bed before sitting down in it. Through tears, runny nose, and sobs, I told the nurse my story. She wiped tears from her own eyes and asked me if I felt safe. Shaking and nervous, I said, "No, I don't."

My bed could be seen from the hallway by anyone who walked past our door. She nodded in agreement, reassuring me that there would always be someone at the desk next to the door and that I could keep my curtain drawn for the entire duration of my stay there. She reminded me that because of the nature of the research for our seizure disorders, my roommate and I were under constant video and audio surveillance.

She brought me a mild sedative to help me sleep. With a reassuring hug, she reminded me and my roommate of our safety. Just then, my sweet roommate said, "Itzabella, I am sorry, but I could not help to overhear your story, and I want you to know that you are the bravest person I have ever met."

I thanked her, and we both drifted off to sleep, sniffling and silently weeping.

Just when I thought I had healed and peeled back all the layers of drama, trauma, and toxicity in my life, out of the blue, this unexpected event presented itself to teach me that I needed to heal another layer.

Through meditation on my intention to rise above all obstacles, to survive and thrive again, I called upon my divine helpers and began another healing journey.

The follow-up appointment with the neurologist revealed that my seizures were nonepileptic. He said that they were related to the stress of suppressing the reality of the traumatic events for so many years, and they were recently multiplied by the trauma associated with seeing Phidelopé again. He wanted me to stay on the epileptic medication to avoid having an epileptic event.

"Rapidly withdrawing from this medication could actually cause epilepsy," he warned.

I was relieved and frustrated at the same time. He also refused to reinstate my driver's license. I felt judged and punished.

His recommendation to see a psychiatrist of his preference was a significant element on my healing journey. At first, I was insulted— that was just my ego working hard to keep me trapped in victim soul mode. I treated myself with self-love and self-care through rest, prayer, meditation, and regular exercise, and I consciously chose to live passionately and purposefully.

In late May 2016, I left the mundane routine of my day-to-day home life and traveled to British Columbia to live with my daughter, son-in-law, and grandson for six weeks. I was happy to help them get through the stress of my grandson's prearranged surgery. I also devoted that time to total self-care, and I prayed daily to release all guilt associated with such a new and selfish decision. I slowly and methodically reduced all prescription medications with the support of daily walks (even in the rain), Bach Flower Remedies, and all natural thyroid supplements. I also followed a natural liver detoxification regimen. I drank hot water with lemon and hot water with apple cider vinegar with a drizzle of pure Canadian maple syrup in it rather than coffee.

As much as I was enthusiastic with this purposeful transition, my body did not readily embrace this change. It retaliated with bouts of migraines and a severe sinus infection that blew out my right eardrum (severe rupture of the tympanic membrane). *Ouch! Ouch! Ouch!*

Thankfully, I healed from those wounds too. I returned home feeling proud of my accomplishments and a little concerned about my ability to continue on this journey to total health. I will admit that I did slip; yet, the consequences of accepting anything less than what is best for my total health quickly persuaded me to get back on track.

Life is good again!

As I surrender my pen and pad of paper, I am thrilled to say that Désirée, Victoria, and Janelle each have one child of their own. They are happy, healthy, brilliant, productive, and confident young women who are lovingly supported by family, friends, and pets.

I now forgive myself for:

- All the times that I accepted less for myself

PEARL OF WISDOM

I am forever grateful for my daily blessings and my answered prayers. Focus on yours, and soon you'll see that you have more and more blessings to be thankful for!